Teaching General Music
in Grades 6–9

Teaching General Music in Grades 6–9

Donald Metz
University of Cincinnati
College-Conservatory of Music

CHARLES E. MERRILL PUBLISHING COMPANY
A Bell & Howell Company
Columbus   Toronto   London   Sydney

Published by
CHARLES E. MERRILL PUBLISHING CO.
A Bell & Howell Company
Columbus, Ohio 43216

This book was set in Helvetica.
Production Editor: Judith Rose Sacks
Cover Design Coordination: Will Chenoweth

Photo Credits
p. 2—Larry Hamill   *pp. 8, 76, 86*—Janus Small   *p. 26*—Students at the National Music Camp, Interlochen, MI. Interlochen photo by Brill   *p. 36*—Courtesy American Music Conference   *p. 52*—E. F. Bernstein Photos   *p. 132*—*Nude Descending A Staircase #2* by Marcel Duchamp. Philadelphia Museum of Art: The Louise and Walter Arensberg Collection

Copyright © 1980 by Bell & Howell Company. All rights reserved. No part of this book may be reproduced in any form, electronic or mechanical, including photocopy, recording, or any information storage and retrieval system, without permission in writing from the publisher.

Library of Congress Catalog Card Number: 79-89595
International Standard Book Number: 0-675-08176-9
Printed in the United States of America
1 2 3 4 5 6 7 8 9 10—85 84 83 82 81 80

Contents

	Preface	vii
1	Developing a Philosophy	3
2	The Curriculum	10
3	Organization and Discipline	27
4	Instruments and Materials	37
5	Classroom Activities	53
6	Lesson Planning	77
7	Sample Lesson Plans	87
8	The Allied Arts	129
	Appendixes	167
	Index	179

Preface

The middle school music class may well be viewed as the most difficult and challenging branch of the school music program. Considering the great variety in attitude, ability, and background of the students, no single text can hope to provide plans and options for every situation. Yet a methods book should allow for differing opinions and approaches. Readers are encouraged to examine as much of the current literature on middle school general music as possible. From these materials, readers may select and build a storehouse of thoughts, approaches, and resources.

This book proceeds on the assumption that the middle school general music teacher-to-be is well grounded in theory, history, and his or her own area of performance. Keyboard skills are essential, not a luxury; guitar and recorder skills are of almost the same importance. College course work on the use of classroom instruments is also important. Above all, a strong desire to share one's enthusiasm for music cannot be valued highly enough.

Philosophy is emphasized in this book because of its central importance to the teaching—learning experience. A teacher must work from some basic beliefs about the importance and purpose of music in order to provide direction, consistency, and insight. The reader is encouraged to focus on the aesthetic aspect of musical experiences in the classroom. The sheer beauty of the musical moment must come before biographies, notebooks, and exams. By spotlighting the musical elements, the teacher can guide students with the enjoyment and excitement that are typical of successful music teachers.

Student teachers should learn how to plan a music lesson. Suggestions are given and plans are provided so that the student has a model to follow. It is hoped that the pressing need for practical, easy-to-follow procedures is partially answered in this book.

Emphasis is given to the "doing" part of the music lesson. Music-making, in any form, certainly will add to the general music program. Even if most students may become observers rather than performers, the class should not be a purely listening, report-writing hour.

The alliance of the arts is a subject that has received renewed interest. As our goal is the further development of the student's artistic awareness, we should welcome the other arts into our classrooms. By broadening the scope of the general music class, both the teacher and the class should profit.

This book has grown out of years of experience in an inner-city junior high school. It is intended to be practical and flexible. Blank pages are included in the lesson plan section (Chapters 7 and 8) for the reader's use. Readers are encouraged to add and delete pages to retain a workable, custom-made body of ideas, references, and plans.

While many students and colleagues provided valuable ideas, suggestions, and contributions, a special acknowledgment is due Dr. Joan K. Lehr, Dr. Kay Reynold, Dr. Mary O'Neil, and Dr. Barbara Andress for their insightful reviews and commentary.

Special appreciation to Josephine Barker and the students at Merry Junior High.

Teaching General Music in Grades 6–9

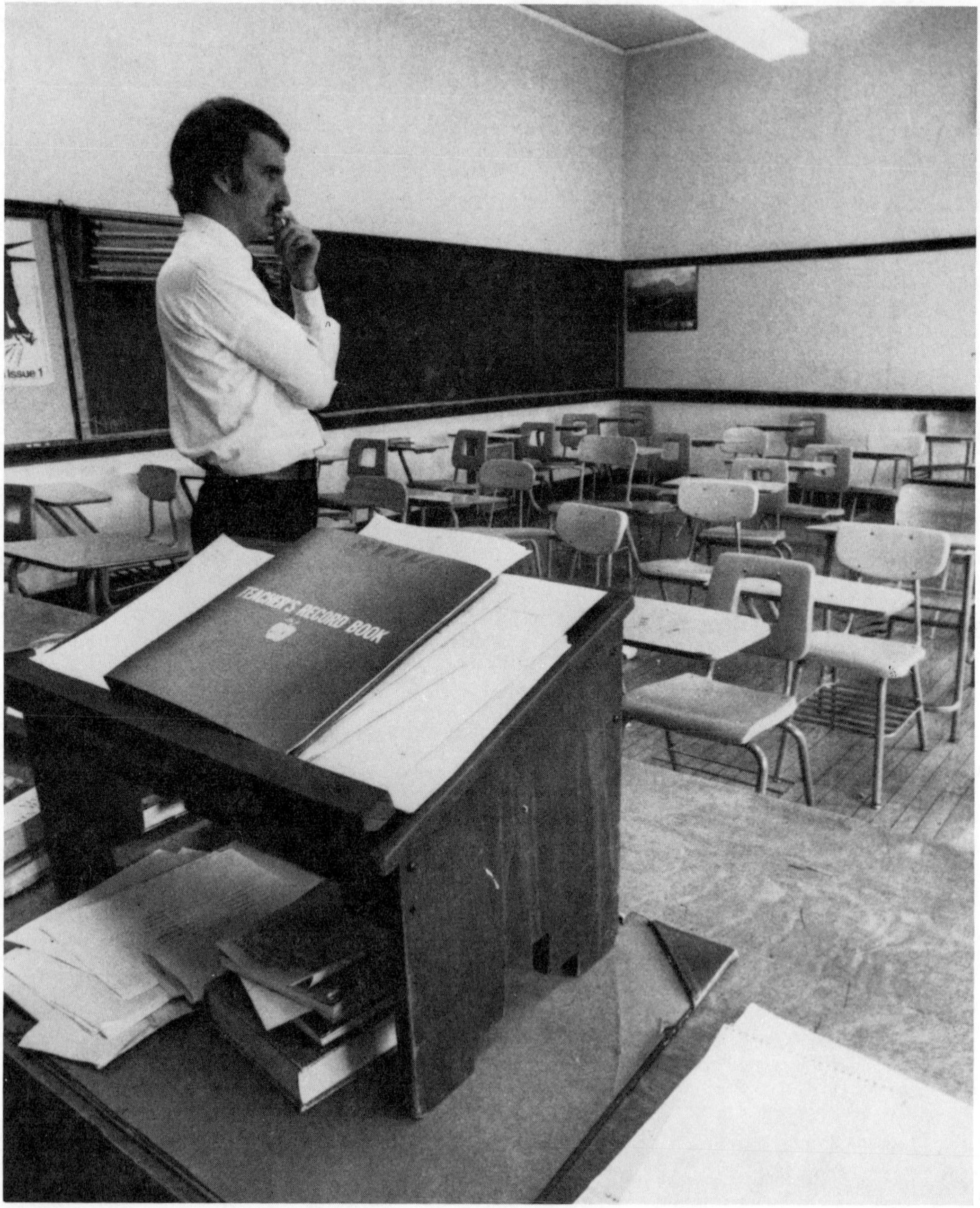
Issue 1
TEACHER'S RECORD BOOK

He who has no port to sail for finds no favorable winds.

Seneca

Developing a Philosophy

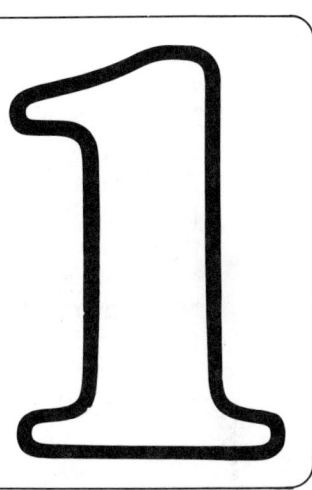

1

Thinking about *what* you do and *why* you do it should be foremost among your duties as a teacher. Some teachers pursue classroom routines without giving thought to long-range goals or to how day-by-day presentations fit into a larger scheme. Music teachers at every level need to stop and take stock of themselves; they should consider what they wish to impart to students and what they believe is most important about their art and craft.

Middle school music classes (grades 6 to 9) consist of groups of students coming from many elementary schools, each with its own level of quality and emphasis of instruction. Further, for most students middle school music will be their last musical experience in a classroom. A music class probably will be large in size—classes with forty to sixty students are not uncommon—with a range of student interest and background. There is great peer pressure. Teachers may find themselves spending most of their class time in bookkeeping, attendance taking, and discipline. It is small wonder that music teachers sometimes seek any shortcut or method that promises active, interested involvement.

Perhaps the heart of the matter lies not in class size or differences in ability, but in the music teacher who doesn't know precisely what to do once attendance is taken and the class is quiet. If the teacher always appears unsettled, rushed, and indecisive, students may respond by maintaining the conditions that cause such behavior. New teachers are likely to deal with challenging student behaviors by placing friendliness—"being one of the gang"—high on their list of good teacher qualities and by agreeing to do whatever the students want to do. These teachers fear that they will lose favor if they act forcefully in class. Students usually are quick to take advantage of such an attitude on the part of the teacher.

How is the teacher to deal with the many factors that contribute to musical progress? Because discipline problems (to be discussed later) often arise in class as a reaction to the teacher's obvious lack of a sense of purpose, the teacher-to-be needs a workable philosophy. The area of philosophy we need to consider is *aesthetics*, for its concerns are our concerns: What is beauty? What is art? What does art do? How do people respond to art? And to which authors should we turn? Meyer has noted some important and current aesthetic theories: Formalism, Referentialism, and Expressionism.[1] Each of these will be discussed briefly and then related to the classroom.

FORMALISM

Formalism is the term for the view that the "formal" qualities of a work of art are most important. The formalist is interested in those features of art that are changeless: balance, design, repetition, contrast, and so forth. Formalists believe that they can, and should, experience art without applying anything from the real world; that art can be approached in terms of craft and style; and that what one gains from such an experience is purely artistic. Personal interpretations and judgments are beside the point, as are titles of works, biographies of the artists, and other knowledge beyond the work itself. Art does not yield mental pictures or specific emotions. The "message" is purely artistic, purely impersonal; for formalists, that message is the "rightness" of a work. Formalism treats art apart from life and apart from human consideration. In its most extreme degree, formalism treats all art not as a human creation or statement but as a "given" to be analyzed and understood.

In the music classroom, the formalist focuses on developing those skills that will help students to become better observers, analysts, and "critics." Such a teacher devotes most of the time to theory, analysis, and listening. Rhythmic and melodic dictation might be used frequently; exercises in elementary composition also would be useful. A formalist could adopt numerous curricular plans, such as a historical approach or an "elements-of-music" design. Whatever the overall plan, the emphasis is on the craft and

---

1. Leonard Meyer, *Emotion and Meaning in Music* (Chicago: The University of Chicago Press, 1956), pp. 1–3.

form of selected musical works—not on biographies, broad social studies-oriented units, or emotional interpretations. Formalists are as energetic, enthusiastic, and convincing as any other type of music teacher. The primary feature of formalists is their deliberate avoidance of any personal/subjective involvement in the creation, performance, or interpretation of musical works.

REFERENTIALISM

Referentialism is the term for the view that artistic elements beyond the work of art itself are centrally important. The who, when, and where of works of art are vital facts for the referentialist. Many who hold to this point of view consider art a kind of language. They seek the message in works of art by attempting to decode and combine all the clues provided by the artist. As a rule, this message can be stated in words; for example, "in this painting the candle stands for the presence of God," or "here, the composer conveys the meaning of his title 'Fog' through these slow-moving, parallel chords." Referentialists do not ignore the internal artistic aspects—the form, balance, textures, repetition, and so on; however, instead of probing only these features deeply (like the formalists), referentialists use these features to help them go beyond to the personal, interpretive realm. Titles, subject matter, or programs provided by artists simplify the task of interpretation. Formulas and symbols in art also help. In sum, referentialists confirm the importance of the emotional power and opportunities for interpretation provided by all art.

In the music classroom, a referential approach is fairly easy to spot. Titled units of study are still prominent: "Music of Our Mexican Neighbors," "Music Paints a Picture," "Sad and Happy Music." Certainly a historic approach is useful, for history can help explain why the music of a given era sounds the way it does. Program music is a favorite; titles and "programs" provide maps for class work. Teachers will often ask their students to draw pictures as a way of interpreting recorded music. Or the teacher might provide several imaginary titles for preselected musical works and ask class members to select the best title. Teachers might tell students to act out some portion of a musical work and then reveal the degree to which the class interpreted the work correctly. Class discussion could include some popular notions of minor mode/sadness, long crescendos/sunrise; how the cloudburst is conveyed musically; and so forth.

Referentialists tend to select "message-oriented" works—nineteenth-century program music, musical works based on other arts, and current film and TV music (including cartoons). Even if a selected work is hard to interpret, a referentialist will make the effort. Music is seen as only partly sound and silence, notes and rests; its primary importance lies in what it means to us, what the composer wanted to tell us, what pictures come to mind, what feelings arise from the music. Teachers who stress the reaction (rather than the perception) of pupils to music and who pepper their speech with descriptive words can be termed referentialist in approach.

EXPRESSIONISM

You might expect the third aesthetic position, Expressionism, to be a middle ground between the other two. This is partly true. Expressionists note the central importance of the structure and qualities of art (like the formalists), while admitting that art is also capable of evoking personal and emotional reactions (like the referentialists). What makes Expressionism unique is its view on the nature of meaning in art.

Expressionism holds that the meaning in art cannot be put into words. Art presents colors, shapes, words, and sounds in deliberately arranged patterns. While each element of any art form may be isolated, examined, and analyzed in light of the whole, the overall meaning is greater than the sum of the parts. That which is conveyed between art and the perceiver is so personal, so private, so delicate that words of interpretation do us no good. All art conveys something, but that "something" is not a clear, precise, verbal message. Expressionism, in admitting the emotional, personal, but wordless impact made by art, thus is distinct from both Formalism and Referentialism.

In the music classroom, the expressionist teacher's task seems more difficult than that of the formalist or referentialist. The expressionist must provide musical experiences that will (*a*) probe the inner workings and relationships of music, and (*b*) help the student to become more sensitive to sound and silence. Expressionists can analyze the purely musical elements with as much vigor as formalists, but such analysis is always coupled with encouragement of aesthetic awareness.

When spotlighting the musical elements alone and in combination, expressionist teachers draw from the music of the Orient, Africa, and the Middle East, along with selections of electronic and chance music. Expressionists place greatest emphasis on *listening* (and learning what to listen for), since this skill is central to every musical activity. Singing, playing instruments, composing, moving, and improvising are important, but they are regarded by expressionists as opportunities for more perceptive listening.

Many musical expressionists believe that the gift of music is "insight," not merely notes and rests and not simply colorful pictures. Music is not "about" any specific thing, yet during perceptive listening we become aware that we feel something. We cannot really put into words what we feel—and expressionists believe we should not try. Instead, we should attend more closely to sounds/silences and feel them as deeply as we can. The more we pay attention, the more we feel. This is the key to the expressionist approach, and at the same time one reason why this philosophy is perhaps the most difficult to put into practice.

Formalists aren't really concerned about interpretation and subjective reaction. Referentialists can turn to descriptive words and graphic aids. But expressionists can only urge their students to let music work upon them, to feel as deeply as they can. A teacher cannot measure the degree to which a young listener feels and reacts to music, however. Students often have been led to believe that music is just scales, key signatures, and definitions or else pictures, colors, and specific moods. The middle school expressionist therefore may have to try to overcome such conditioning in the students' musical backgrounds.

Despite its potential problems, Expressionism appears to be the philosophy that promises the most for music education. Like Formalism, it respects the art and craft of music; like Referentialism, it admits the existence and importance of the subjective impact in music. Expressionism never attempts to be overly clinical or overly interpretive. Rather, it adopts in a unique way the best of the various available points of view.

Questions & Activities

1. How does having a philosophy of music education make you a better teacher?
2. Divide the class into three groups of equal size. Using the same materials (records or songs), have each group teach a short lesson illustrating (a) the formalistic, (b) the referential, or (c) the expressionistic approach. Have the class discuss the strengths and weaknesses of the three philosophies as applied in the classroom.
3. Examine selected books or other materials and attempt to discover their underlying philosophy. Choose from standard published series, texts on junior high school music, and available curricula from local school systems.

Junior High
MUSIC
JUNIOR
HIGH SCHOOL
GENERAL MUSIC
Folk Music in School
Listen!
SILVER BURDETT
music
Teacher's Edition

There are two kinds of fools: one says, "This is old, therefore it is good"; the other says, "This is new, therefore it is better."

William Ralph Inge

The Curriculum 2

Philosophy refers to the basic beliefs you hold about the purpose and value of music in education; *curriculum* has to do with the way in which that philosophy is put into action. The curriculum includes all the features of the music program: the goals, plans, timetables, selections, and activities. It spells out how and what the students will experience musically in your class.

School systems differ in terms of size, traditions, equipment, and interest. Some systems have strong music programs with active supervisors and well-planned experiences. Often, however, there is no supervisor to tell you what to do and when to do it; the musical activities and programs in your school depend on *you*.

The history of American education has shown a split in opinion about the value of musical activity. Should music be regarded more for the nonmusical benefits supposedly associated with it—improving mental health, building discipline, and the like—or for its own value? Over time, educators have become more aware that the primary importance of music is its aesthetic power and value. This is especially true for the general music program. The development of students' aesthetic sensitivity is the central focus of this book. We shall now examine some of the ways of translating this belief into action. Figure 2.1 shows the path from philosophy to application in the classroom.

FIGURE 2.1

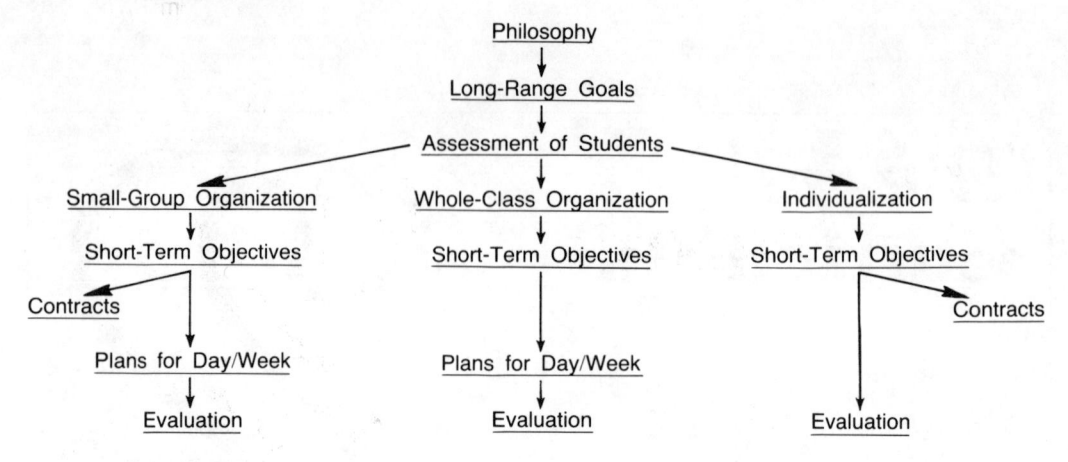

```
                        Philosophy
                            ↓
                      Long-Range Goals
                            ↓
            ┌───────  Assessment of Students  ───────┐
            ↓               ↓                        ↓
  Small-Group Organization  Whole-Class Organization  Individualization
            ↓               ↓                        ↓
    Short-Term Objectives   Short-Term Objectives   Short-Term Objectives
       ↙                                                    ↘
  Contracts                                                  Contracts
       ↓                    ↓                                ↓
  Plans for Day/Week    Plans for Day/Week
       ↓                    ↓                                ↓
    Evaluation           Evaluation                      Evaluation
```

As we look at the middle school general music curriculum, attention will be directed first to developing long-range goals. Once goals are decided on and the musical abilities of the class have been assessed, the teacher can then choose the most suitable form of curriculum organization. No single approach is best in every situation; therefore, a variety of options—and their strengths and drawbacks—will be presented.

LONG-RANGE GOALS

There is quite a difference between vague, general goals and goals that are well-defined and observable. "All students should learn to love music" is a goal that is admirable but is not concrete or capable of being measured. "All students should be able to sing a simple melody in tune" is clearer and measurable. Formulating classroom goals, selecting approaches, planning the actual activities and experiences, and designing good testing methods all are to the advantage of the teacher. Laying the groundwork actually frees the teacher to enjoy more fully the work in class.

Areas of Musical Learning

"I'm the last music teacher these kids will ever have. What do I want them to experience? What is it I can leave with them that will help them musically? How can I stir interest in music beyond rock music radio stations and occasional ticket purchases for pop music star performances? In brief, how can my music class make a difference? What is most important?" These are central, realistic questions you might find yourself asking. To find the answers, we can begin by looking at the different categories or areas of musical learning. Three such areas may be defined briefly as follows:

Cognitive:	mental-verbal (knowledge) "the student can verbalize, perceive, classify, recall . . ."
Motor:	performance (skill) "the student can sing, tap, clap, move, play . . ."
Affective:	emotional, attitudinal (sensitivity) "the student shows interest, actively pursues, displays approach behavior. . . ."

Too much attention to any one area may work against the other two. For example, to spend every class hour on the facts, dates, names, and terms of music without also giving attention to motor and affective behaviors would limit severely the scope of the class. Finding the best blend of all three behavior categories is quite a challenge. Let us now examine some goals suggested for junior high general music, listed within the various areas.

Cognitive Area

1. knowledge of and experience with music's basic elements—melody, harmony, rhythm, texture, timbre, dynamics, and form—alone and in combinations
2. ability (*a*) to listen attentively and carefully, and (*b*) to identify formal aspects, from motif/phrase to differentiating larger whole parts
3. knowledge of leading composers, specific works, and styles from the seventeenth century to the present
4. ability to identify the terms and signs used in both traditional and avant-garde notation
5. knowledge by sight and by ear of the various tone-producing instruments (orchestral, vocal, and electronic). Recognition by ear is central; visual recognition, though helpful, is less important.

Motor Area

1. *singing* (both by rote and by note) simple melodies and ostinati with accuracy in pitch and duration
2. *playing* keyboard, fretted, and classroom instruments
3. *listening* to students' own work and to recorded/live music, with purposeful, focused perception

4. *moving* to music: clapping, conducting, tapping, and dancing
5. *creating* short pieces, from simple, improvised phrases and ostinati to songs and instrumental compositions

Affective Area

1. demonstrating growth in musical value judgments
2. showing a more positive attitude toward music
3. applying skills gained in class to new musical experiences
4. tolerating the taste and values of others
5. displaying an increased willingness to participate in classroom activities
6. demonstrating performance sensitivity to even simple routines and experiences in class

ASSESSMENT OF STUDENTS

In order to plan the right kinds of musical activities for the class, the teacher must determine the level of students' knowledge and experience. Every class has its own needs, and so plans cannot be proposed that will work all the time for all students. Similarly, a plan that works for someone else should not be copied automatically—it might not work at all for *your* needs. The weeks and months you share with students at this stage of their schooling are very precious. It is important that you waste no time covering things students already know; also avoid leaping into areas for which they have no preparation.

Your assessment of students will be influenced by your view of what is important. If you apply a formalist philosophy, you will want to (*a*) find out the extent of the students' knowledge of symbols, names, and dates; (*b*) spend your first week giving rhythmic and melodic dictation; and (*c*) provide opportunities for students to demonstrate their skills in formal analysis. Performance skills, such as singing and playing classroom instruments, may or may not be central to the formalist's assessment.

On the other hand, if you are a referentialist, you probably will want to determine the students' ability to put into words their reactions to music. You might choose a number of programmatic works to play and then ask for "appropriate" responses. Drawing pictures might be in order, if verbal skills are limited. Attitudes are important to you (far more than performance skills); you might ask students which pieces they liked best. Or you might approach assessment by providing a story or poem and asking for a suitable musical setting. In any case, facts and knowledge are less important to you than emotional and social responses.

Expressionists recognize the importance of both parts of the aesthetic experience—the *perception* of musical events and the *reaction* to them. Expressionists are quick to point out, however, that the personal reaction should be left alone; to tamper with it, by proposing "appropriate" moods or pictures, does a disservice to the music and to the gradual expansion of pupils' artistic training. Expressionists focus on improving perception, because it is the teachable part of the musical experience. Assessment of pupils closely resembles the formalist's approach in that it deals with musical aspects only. A wide variety of music (both Western and Oriental) may well be chosen to provide the best examples for perceptual analysis. Questions will be carefully worded to *avoid* an interpretive slant (such as "Is the melody happy or sad?"). Expressionists are interested in charting progress of students as they hear and react to music. Students may be questioned about where phrases start and end, where a new section begins, and so on.

Having assessed the students' general abilities, the teacher must budget class time wisely; a great deal will have to be done in a short time. Your philosophy can help you sort out what is important to accomplish and what is not. Following is a sample assessment test that could be used at the beginning of the year. The test takes into account the fact that some students may have begun private study and may already be well grounded in basic music skills and terms.

MUSICAL ASSESSMENT TEST: GRADE____

Name _____ Age_____ Date_____
Elementary school attended _____
Private lessons on (instrument)_____for_____years

1. In front of the name of each instrument, place the initial of the family it belongs to.
   S = string family; **WW** = woodwind; **B** = brass; **P** = percussion

   _____drum   _____violin   _____clarinet   _____trumpet
   _____viola   _____tuba   _____triangle   _____flute
   _____bassoon   _____oboe   _____trombone   _____cello

2. In the following short musical example, use the ⊙▶ to point out the following parts:
   Ⓐ▶ melody
   Ⓑ▶ harmony
   Ⓒ▶ time signature
   Ⓓ▶ key signature

3. What does ———— mean? _____
   What does $\frac{3}{4}$ mean? _____
   What do these mean?
      p _____
      $f\!f$ _____
      ⌢ _____
      :‖ _____

4. List any composers' names you remember from elementary school, even if you do not know the exact spelling.
   _____
   _____
   _____
   _____
   _____

5. Shown here are groups of notes. I'll play the notes, but I'll change one of them. You circle the note I change.

   A   B   C   D

6. On the following list, circle the correct musical event as I call the letter. I will repeat the piece if necessary.
   Selection: *(your choice; something direct, clear, and relatively obvious)*
   A. melody is jumpy——or——melody is smooth.
   B. violin solo——or——flute solo——or——bassoon solo
   C. rhythm is in 2's (2/4);——or——in 3's (3/4)

7. Shown below are four rhythm patterns; which one am I playing on the drum? Circle the letter of the pattern you hear. *(These could be expanded to fit your needs. Avoid overly complex patterns.)*

   A

   B

   C

   D

8. I'll play this melody three times; first, as written. Second, I'll stop on one of the tones. **Circle the note I stop on and put a 1 over it.** Third, I'll play the melody and change one of the tones. **Circle the changed tone and put a 2 over it.**

9. Following is the rhythm pattern of a familiar melody. Figure out what the tune is, then put in
   A. the correct time signature (2/4 or 3/4 or 4/4) and
   B. the bar lines where they belong.

10. Name your three favorite music albums. _____

    How many records do you own? _____
    List names of concerts you have attended. _____

    What was your **most enjoyable** musical experience? _____

    What was your **least enjoyable** musical experience? _____

Such a test can be shortened or enlarged to suit your needs. Read through each question carefully with the students so that you are certain they understand what you want done.

SHORT-TERM OBJECTIVES

Short-term objectives are those ends we seek after a unit of work or after one day's activities. Given the importance commonly placed upon the behavioral approach, our short-term objectives will be largely observable and measurable. Skills taught also should be musically purposeful. For example, it is less important that a student can parrot "Bach's dates are 1685 to 1750" than that he or she can improvise upon an ostinato in a Baroque style.

Short-term objectives force you to limit yourself and to be precise. They are sometimes cast in formula style: "After one week of melodic dictation, students will be able to (a)_____, (b)_____, and (c)_____." They are really nothing more than written expectations. It is very difficult to evaluate the students' progress if you have not decided upon relatively clear-cut objectives.

Let us use one musical element, melody, to examine how one might develop some short-term objectives. This example can then be extended to other elements. What is important for middle school students to grasp about melody? Should they study the Locrian mode? Chances are you will rule out Locrian mode because it is too remote, not really essential. In so doing, you have made a decision. What about melodic and harmonic minor—should all students know the difference? What of non-Western and nontraditional scales? As you select and discard, you see the need to have a philosophy against which to consider such possibilities. Could you pick and choose *without* any basic belief? Yes, but your choices would be based more on whim than on reasoning.

What *is* essential about melody? Probably, it is a grasp of the melodic line as a whole. In approaching a whole melody, we must attend to how the line is built, through motif and phrases. Scales and modes also can be included here, not as formulas to memorize and reproduce but as tools for organizing groups of tones. Tonal "magnetism" is essential; one can explore how this works in various scales and how it is *not* in effect in, say, a whole-tone scale. The point here is that we would focus upon the sound patterns and how they affect us, rather than on their theoretical structure.

Another consideration would be the contour of a melody, that is, the general shape of a line. Can we trace (on the board, on paper, in the air) the shape of a given phrase? Is the contour smooth and flowing, or angular and jagged? Does the contour itself convey a feeling? What would happen if we changed parts of the contour—would it have the same effect?

Does a short linear graph on the blackboard of a given melody help the ear follow the rise and fall?

Notation as a study in itself is not essential; however, many classes find the various historical approaches to notation quite interesting. Some classes enjoy the challenge of inventing their own notation schemes. Such a project should be examined in class, with strengths and problems pointed out.

By deciding what is most important for students to know about melody, a teacher can more easily determine how to use the time spent on melody. Teachers would plan class time so that opportunities are provided for the following:

1. seeing and hearing the shape or contour of melody
2. exploring motif and phrase as melodic building blocks
3. seeing, hearing, and creating complete melodies
4. discussing various scales and modes used by composers
5. investigating the function of and variation in notation styles

Once the central objectives have been arrived at, you can begin to select the best melodic examples to hear, look at, perform, and discuss. First, turn to what you have sung or played or heard—to things you already know well. A second source might be any of the "music appreciation" books available. Most recent books of this type are organized around musical elements; almost all of them have lists of melodies that are jagged/smooth, high/low, long/short, major/minor, and so on. Many will even indicate where you can locate the respective melody—part, movement, symphony. Third, consider anthologies or collections such as the *Historical Anthology of Music*.[1] If you seek a particular melodic pattern, consult the *Dictionary of Musical Themes*.[2] The *Dictionary* has hundreds of vocal and instrumental themes, both in original form and transposed to the key of C. Fourth, consider popular/folk/non-Western music. "Top 40" ballads are often good choices for melodic examples. Fifth, most schools own some graded music book series.

Decide whether some audiovisual aids can be used. Tracing patterns onto clear acetate with a felt-tip pen and then projecting the patterns by an overhead apparatus might work. A metal clothes hanger could be stretched out into a desired shape and then decorated with styrofoam balls strung along the wire to represent notes.

---

1. Archibald Davison and Willi Apel, *Historical Anthology of Music*, two vols. (Cambridge, Mass.: Harvard University Press, 1956–1957).
2. Harold Barlow and Sam Morgenstern, *A Dictionary of Musical Themes* (New York: Crown, 1957).

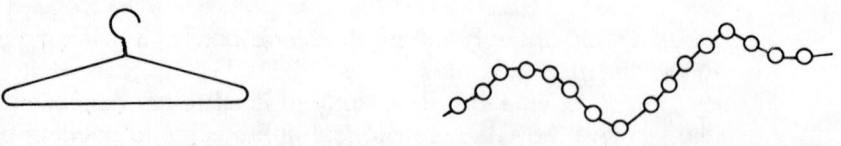

The old standby, the blackboard, can be approached imaginatively. Try tracing contours with the flat side of the chalk.

The same approach used with melody may be applied to the other musical elements. What is and is not essential for your students to know about rhythm? Should all students be expected to tap 3 against 2 on their desks? If you rule this out, do you know why? Limit your list of important concepts to those that should be part of everyone's musical education and those that can be dealt with realistically in class.

The scope of music is vast. Teachers who attempt to cover everything may do a disservice to students and to music. Aim for the basics; stress the idea that students can enjoy and succeed in musical activities; promote positive attitudes about music by showing students how they can continue their musical involvement after they leave your class. By limiting your focus, you free yourself and your classes to explore the magic of music in depth.

Parcelling Out the Work

Now you are faced with the task of organizing your work. Some teachers begin the year by saying, "Class, we'll start with melody and when you have learned what you should, we'll move on to something else." No two classes will arrive at that magic moment at the same time, however; this method also gives no assurance that all concepts will be dealt with as fully as they need to be. Another teacher takes a different tack: "Hurry up and learn these scales, because Friday is our last day on melody. After that we'll be doing something different." This teacher has structured the content by the calendar, and woe to him or her who falls behind.

Music teachers, like all teachers, face two problems: the breadth of the subject matter and the differing abilities of students. Which is more important, covering subject matter or teaching students? Clearly, the latter. But you cannot spend all year waiting for students to live up to your expectations in a certain area; nor can you simply divide the number of class days by topics to be covered and expect good results. How, then, to plan?

UNIT PLANS vs. THE SPIRAL CURRICULUM

As we look further at day-by-day planning, it may be helpful to note an ineffective method which should be avoided. A widespread "plan" is the *non-plan.* By this we mean the absence of any systematic approach—a seemingly random selection of content and experiences. Teachers who have a non-plan may feel that they *can't* plan because their students are unmotivated, unpredictable, and "only passing through." Songs will be sung and records played, but without a focus or sense of purpose.

A variation of the non-plan is seen in the teacher who asks, "Well, what would you like to do today?" Those who favor this approach claim that it honors the students' interests and that it allows students to control the shape and content of the class. But the teacher who has no specific musical goals will have trouble in the long run. Middle school students cannot fairly be expected to know what should be done in a general music class. If you structure the class only around what students know and like, you may be dealing with quite a limited range of pop/rock music.

A better approach, and the one that is the most frequently found, is to organize the class around the music series textbook used by the school. Years ago, such books were basically song collections. Today, a variety of approaches is apparent. Some books cling to the song approach and attempt to update their method by including many rock/pop songs. But most publishers now organize their books into units of work. A look at the tables of contents of a couple of recent textbooks reveals some trends in publishing.

Exploring Music, Grade 7

The Gift of Song
What is Music?
Pop Songs From the Top Forty
Music All Around You
Johann Sebastian Bach, the Composer for All Time
Patterns and Designs: Polyphonic Music
Bela Bartok and His Music
Communicating Musical Ideas
Franz Liszt and His Music
Sounds of Drums
Music from the Far East
Music and Dance in Africa
Music from Regions of the West
Johannes Brahms and His Music
Ludwig van Beethoven and His Music
Music by Chance
Patterns and Designs: Sonata Allegro

Unit Plans vs. The Spiral Curriculum

>Patterns and Designs: the Concerto
>Patterns and Designs: the Symphony
>Patterns and Designs: the Overture
>Standard Designs in Music
>American Folk Songs Today and Yesterday
>West Side Story
>Your Career in Music
>The Changing Styles in Music
>More Songs to Sing
>Revolutionary Ideas, Part II [3]

>*Sound, Beat, and Feeling*
>Sound, Beat, and Feeling
>Music and You
>Understanding Rhythm and Color
>Exploring Line, Texture, and Design
>Playing Instruments
>Ethnic Worlds
>Temporal Worlds
>Music for Chorus [4]

As can be seen, fewer songs are included today. Contemporary sounds are included; musical elements and concepts are emphasized; activities for playing/improvising are included; non-Western music is also there. Clearly, the middle school music class is no longer a singing session. Musical elements are given the most emphasis, with singing considered only a part of the program.

Many middle school students remember very little from their elementary music classes—a few songs, perhaps the autoharp, and pictures of orchestral instruments. Now look again at those tables of contents. The teacher must evaluate the published materials, adapting and borrowing those musical ideas and suggestions that are appropriate for the class.

---

3. From Beth Landis, *Exploring Music, Grade 8* (New York: Holt, Rinehart and Winston, 1975), pp. ii–iii. Used with permission.
4. From Robert A. Choate, Barbara Kaplan, and James Standifer, *Sound, Beat, and Feeling, Grade 7* (New York: American Book Company, 1976), p. v. Used with permission.

The Unit Plan

Experienced general music teachers frequently use the *unit plan*. They arrange the course around large units of work and turn to the textbook only as needed. Units are chosen with an eye on both student interests and the calendar. Usually, each unit has a title given it and all work done within a unit relates to the general theme. Bessom, Tatarunis, and Forcucci have devised a plan for a listening class that is frequently borrowed for general music:[5]

Unit	Approx. Portion of 36-Week Course

I. The Elements of Music
   A. Dimensions of tone
   B. Basic elements
   C. Design elements
   D. Performance media and interpretation
	3 weeks

II. Popular Music
   A. The rise of popular music in America
   B. Basic styles from Tin Pan Alley to rock
   C. Music analysis of the pop–rock idiom
	3 weeks

III. Classical Music
   A. Early music through the Renaissance
   B. Baroque music
   C. Rococo and preclassical music
   D. Music of the classical period
   E. Romanticism and postromanticism
   F. Music of the twentieth century
	17 weeks

IV. Jazz
   A. General characteristics
   B. Traditional jazz styles
   C. Big-band styles
   D. Modern jazz styles
	4 weeks

V. Folk and Ethnic Music
   A. The oral tradition
   B. Ethnic musics of the United States
   C. Musics of Oceania
   D. Musics of Northeast Asia
   E. Musics of Southeast Asia
   F. Musics of South Asia
   G. Musics of West Asia–North Africa
	4 weeks

---

5. From *Teaching Music in Today's Secondary Schools: A Creative Approach to Contemporary Music Education* by Malcolm E. Bessom, Alphonse M. Tatarunis and Samuel L. Forcucci. Copyright © 1974 by Holt, Rinehart and Winston, Inc. Reprinted by permission of Holt, Rinehart and Winston.

Unit Plans vs. The Spiral Curriculum

Unit	Approx. Portion of 36-Week Course
H. Musics of Africa south of the Sahara	4 weeks
I. Folk musics of Europe	
J. Musics of North, Central, and South America	
VI. Music Theatre	2 weeks
A. Operetta	
B. Musical comedy	
C. Musical play	
VII. Synthesis: A Review of Music Materials	3 weeks
A. Rhythm	
B. Melody	
C. Harmony	
D. Form	
E. Performance media	
F. Interpretation	
G. Style	

Units, by their very nature, divide the year's work into relatively manageable parts. They attempt to provide variety, and they can be chosen with the seasons in mind. There can be as few or as many units as necessary. And units provide a timetable for teacher and students. As a curricular plan, there is nothing really wrong with units. The chief drawback of the unit plan is that it forces the teacher to limit the focus to a main topic or theme. One could spend a month on a topic to the exclusion of everything else. During that month, every song, record, activity, and experience would be chosen with the main theme in mind. For example, if you select *melody* as a unit of work, study materials would be boundless. But if you were to select "Songs of Our Argentinean Neighbors" as a unit, the scope and variety would be very limited.

Unit organization has another drawback. Using a typical unit plan assumes that students will study one topic for a while and then move on to another, perhaps unrelated, topic. After a class studies conducting patterns, for example, for a week, they study African dances—never to return to conducting patterns. This approach lacks a core of study that requires consistent and frequent review and exploration. Dividing the music work into short, different units may be convenient for the teacher. But it may not be the most logical or effective organization for musical learning.

The unit plan has many supporters—and many opponents. It can be handled easily and efficiently, or with unthinking reliance on schedules and timetables. Let this suggestion guide you: Use whatever plan is most comfortable, so long as the content and method spotlight that which is *musical*.

The Spiral Curriculum

The *spiral* (or *cyclic*) *curriculum* has been proposed as perhaps the ideal structure for music education. In brief, the spiral curriculum rests on the idea that within a given field of study there are *basic concepts* that remain central to the study and understanding of that field. These basic concepts are so significant, so vital that one could not possibly deal adequately with them in a single lesson. In analyzing a great symphony or painting, a student always learns more about it with repeated exposure, simply because the work has so much to give. Therefore, it is not appropriate to divide work into unrelated units. No matter how many units one could devise, music should be studied in light of the basic concepts—regardless of where, when, or how the music developed. For example, rock music is music *first*, and a popular style second. Those who favor the spiral curriculum admit that it is perhaps the most difficult kind of organization to put into practice. It lacks a well-ordered timetable that takes into account the variety of students' interests and abilities; yet it proposes that students should study music by returning to basic concepts.

Ideally, a spiral curriculum should be what the term suggests: an unbroken thread spinning about its core in ever-widening spirals. Materials and activities should be selected according to whether they will promote musical insight and feeling. Musical examples should reveal or relate to basic musical concepts. The entire focus is upon how sound and silence are used; thus, there is no separate unit on rock or African rhythms or Greek modes.

A Simple Spiral Curriculum

Given the differences from area to area in school vacations and holidays, you can plan for about thirty-six weeks of annual work in the public school. These weeks may be divided into semesters, quarters, or modules. Nonmusical factors have an important bearing on how you will divide your time. For example, if your school year has two semesters, and your students are required to take only one semester, your actual work will be compressed to one half. In this case you would arrange your classes around an eighteen-week sequence (for example, from Labor Day to Christmas); you would then repeat the plan, with certain changes, from New Year's to summer vacation. Let us assume this is the plan you inherit. How shall the work be organized?

Following the basic philosophy encouraged in this book, you will direct your students' attention primarily toward those elements that turn sound and silence into music: melody, rhythm, harmony, texture, tone color, and form (your terms may include pitch, duration, amplitude, timbre, and so on). All of these elements combine in musical compositions. The job ahead is

Unit Plans vs. The Spiral Curriculum

to develop students' ability to focus on one element, then on two, and so on until they can focus on several elements in combination. If you are lucky enough to get a class that is well trained and broadly experienced, then your plan should begin at a more advanced level.

As the musical elements constitute the heart of the spiral program, let us chart a rough plan around them:

Weeks	Topic
1–3	melody
4–6	rhythm
7–9	tone color and texture
10–12	harmony
13–15	form
16–18	historic and idiomatic styles

This plan is too unitlike; it allows equal time to all elements, with no evidence of continuity from elementary school. It also fails to take into account the most important feature of spiral structure—repetition. So, let's take the plan (still based on the eighteen-week idea) one step further:

Weeks	Topic
1–2	Review; melody
3–5	melody and rhythm
6–8	melody, rhythm, tone color and texture
9–12	melody, rhythm, tone color, texture, and harmony
13–14	all the above, plus form
15–18	all elements as stylistic features

Here, the time spans have been juggled to account for areas that may require more or less attention. As it stands, it is workable, and it does contain a pattern of musical "threads" that stay in the course content. Note that melody, for example, remains an ingredient right from the first week. As one progresses through the half year, melodies (or rhythms or any of the other elements) will return, but each time with new value, in a new light. A symphonic theme is examined during the first week as an example of step-wise motion; during Week 3, the students hear the same theme again, but this time they clap its rhythm. During the eighth week, one attends to the timbre of the solo instrument that plays the theme; perhaps in the sixteenth week, the melody returns to be studied as a smooth, contoured melody typical of the Classical period.

The spiral structure, shown here in "bare bones" form, can be altered by (*a*) shifting the order of the elements or (*b*) changing the amount of time spent on each element. The important features of the plan are (*a*) to keep the focus *musical* at all times, (*b*) to gradually increase the complexity of the tasks, and (*c*) to return continually to past experiences. The process is slow; it requires extensive assessment and planning; the teacher must have solid knowledge of a variety of musics; the plan requires patience and steadfastness. But of all the approaches, *the spiral curriculum appears to be the most relevant, the most suitable, the most musical.*

Yet even the plan shown earlier is not the very best arrangement. First, teachers who keep in touch with the elementary schools believe that a spiral approach should reinforce the elementary experiences. Second, if the early weeks concentrate on melody, for example, the other elements should not be overlooked entirely until the scheduled time. Third, rhythmic patterns, instrument identification, and simple experiments with form should be included regularly, along with listening opportunities and creative tasks. No curriculum formula is perfect; the challenge is to manage time and emphasis so as to best serve the needs of the students.

Questions & Activities

1. Make a list of long-term goals for middle school general music that you feel are essential. Plan your list around the major areas of any music program—cognitive, affective, and motor. What should all middle school graduates know about and be able to do with music?
2. Choosing any *one* long-term goal, develop a series of short-term objectives which you feel will lead to that goal.
3. Focus on one small area or concept you think is important to pursue. Draw up some specific plans to explore this area or concept.

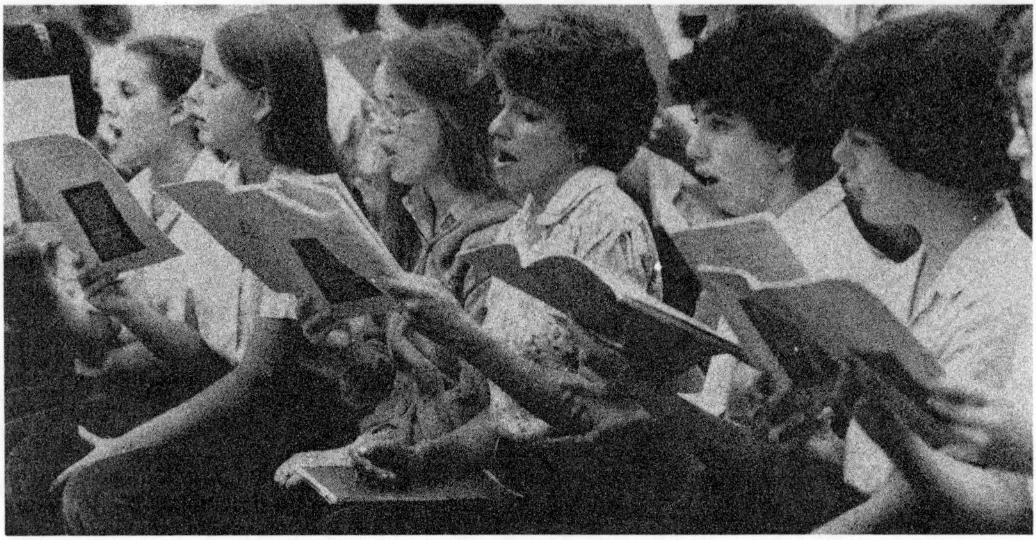

Children have more need of models than of critics.

Joseph Joubert

Organization and Discipline 3

No matter what your philosophy is, you should consider the strengths and weaknesses of some of the ways of grouping students in your classes. Our concern will be with the three most widely used groupings: whole class, small groups, and individualization. Certain activities and projects call for specific arrangements of students for the best results. Therefore, the teacher cannot always rely upon only one way of grouping.

WHOLE-CLASS ARRANGEMENT

Teaching all of the class at once is the traditional approach. Students sit and watch you. Some rooms seem to be designed for this approach. The whole-class approach traces its origin to the lecture format, in which the teacher tells and students take notes (or respond, or sing, or clap, or discuss). For lessons that are lectures, the whole-class approach is fine. It can work with other musical activities, but sometimes there is a problem—the efficient management of people, instruments, and materials as they move from point to point in the room.

A very attractive feature of this approach is that the teacher needs to prepare only *one* presentation, since all students receive the same lesson at the same time. Teachers try to aim their lesson "down the middle"—not too easy, not too hard. The teacher hopes that the brighter, more interested students will pull along the slower, less involved students. Serious problems arise, however, when students become bored with unchallenging presentations or when some of the students feel defeated by the success of higher-achieving students.

The whole-class approach may not be the most effective for every class every day. We may depend on it, though, for the following basic musical activities:

1. group singing
2. listening lessons
3. instrumental activities using many instruments
4. some allied arts lessons

SMALL-GROUP APPROACH

This approach takes into account the differences among students in any music class. On the basis of your assessment test, suppose you find that out of thirty students, five have had private instrumental lessons and enjoy classical music; seventeen students have had no private lessons, but they enjoy singing and own some records; and eight students have had no lessons, cannot read notes, own no records, and don't seem to care. Recognizing that common goals for this class may not be realistic, you divide the class into three groups. During the week, the whole class might meet twice for group singing, dances, and to discuss certain musical points. Each group would spend the rest of the week working on its own—working on problems and activities geared to its interests and abilities. Small groups can work on their own easily if rooms are large enough to permit good separation. Practice rooms and offices can be used if isolation is necessary.

The small-group approach requires clear, thorough planning by the teacher. Activities and assignments must be devised so that groups do not require the teacher's constant attention and control. Low-achievement groups pose the greatest drawback to this approach; without any peer leadership, these group members are likely to "tread water" at best.

The major shortcoming of the small-group approach is that it tends to further separate and isolate groups that are already dissimilar. Keep in mind, too, the power of peer pressure among these students; music class should not encourage the forming of in-groups. On the other hand, small groups are ideal for:

1. small vocal/instrumental ensemble work
2. rehearsing separate accompaniments
3. project work
4. work in specific areas of study

INDIVIDUALIZATION

This educational approach has been applied in music since the 1950s. It found immediate favor in courses that were primarily verbal and analytical. General music, however, largely has avoided this approach. One might feel that training in art is a personal, private matter best handled by individualization. But wholesale adoption of this strategy is far from being a realistic choice. No teacher has the time to create hundreds of tailor-made curricula, nor are school rooms designed for this approach. Nevertheless, there are times when individualized instruction in music seems appropriate:

1. any creative activity (composition, movement, and so on)
2. independent research or study projects
3. remedial work

So long as education is funded by the public, officials will seek ways to make instruction more efficient for the masses. Small-group work and individualized instruction deal with small numbers of students, and so the whole-class approach is most widely used. Such policy is understandable. However, the music teacher should use a variety of class groupings, selected on the basis of what suits the instructional need.

Whether you deal with a class of sixty, or a general class broken into small subgroups, or one thirteen-year-old trying to write an original melody, your goals remain the same: better listening, better appreciation, better grasp of musical techniques. Attention to these concerns is the *one* constant in every good program of music education. Music must become a living thing—an aspect of life that adds something magical and rewarding, and without which life would simply be less meaningful.

Contracts

Evaluation of students has long been a problem for the mindful teacher. Teachers face hundreds of students weekly, with schedules changing frequently. Some teachers avoid the whole issue of evaluation by stating that as long as the student attends class and is quiet and obedient, he or she will receive an A. If the student misbehaves or cuts class frequently, the grade will be lowered accordingly. Obviously, such a method pays no attention to the students' growth in musical interest and sensitivity. *Good* teachers, however, always plan ways to observe and help individual class members. Good teachers take student evaluation seriously. Like classroom arrangements and ways to organize the curriculum, methods for evaluation have become more varied.

Contracts have become popular in recent years, especially in middle school general music.[1] Contracts are simply statements of intent made by students. Usually these contracts take the form of one-page checklists in which the students, either singly or in a small group, contract with the teacher to do certain musical tasks. The teacher can either supply the class with a list of acceptable musical experiences or allow students free rein in their choices. A time limit usually is established, and the student(s) signs the contract. Once all pupils have been contracted, students use class time to pursue their choices. Near the end of certain grading periods, special days are set up—contract days—so that each student or small group can show the rest of the class what he/she/they have done. Some contracts even permit the student to select the letter grade for which he or she is aiming. There are strengths to this option, but also drawbacks.

Contract arrangements work best when one is dealing with large rooms, plentiful equipment and resources, and motivated students. The advantage of contracts is that they are specific, for both student and teacher. The goals of the work are stated. Deadlines help prevent wasting time. Interested parents can be told of their children's work in a very matter-of-fact matter. Students who fail to abide by the contract know well in advance that their grade will be lowered drastically. Contracts thus are relatively clear-cut, and they make grading much easier.

Contracts, however, should not be used simply because they are a convenience. Further, individual contracts fail to take into account the social values of music. All middle school students need the opportunity to share the power of music in a large-group setting—singing songs, playing instruments, and folk dancing. Many musical experiences are best handled with the class as a whole. Too often, contract arrangements end up with many students spread out into halls and corners, each working alone. One might compare this with a Physical Education class in which students never participate in group games or sports but instead choose to learn and write down the rules of several sports for a grade.

If you do decide to use the contract plan, be aware of its limitations. Select experiences or tasks that will help your students now and

---

1. For further discussion of the preparation of musical contracts, consult the Suggested Readings at the end of this chapter.

in the future. Design the tasks to be (*a*) musically meaningful and (*b*) related to a variety of abilities. Thus, it would be proper to suggest this contract statement:

> "Within one week, I promise to research and report (in written form) on the life of Scarlatti. The paper will be typed and will include information about his life and compositions."
> (signed by student) _____
>
> (date) _____

But the final report probably would be little more than reworded information taken from a well-known source. In addition, this contract does not require that the student *hear* any of Scarlatti's compositions.

Consider, instead, something along these lines:

> "Bob, Alice, and I will make some simple instruments out of scrap materials. We will then compose a 'sound-piece' and perform it for the class by November_____."

or

> "Bill and I will take two compositions— 'Hey Jude' by the Beatles and 'Carillon' from Bizet's *L'Arlesienne Suite, No. 1*—and prepare a class discussion and listening lesson on the concept and use of repetition. We shall play both works and prepare listening guides for the rest of the class members."

or

> "Using some slides my parents took during their trip to England, I'll prepare a short talk about English cathedrals. To incorporate some music, I'll include Purcell's 'Trumpet Voluntary' recorded on the organ at Westminster Abbey."

or

> "Using five tone bars, Mary and I will invent a

pentatonic ostinato which can be used to accompany our singing of 'An Iroquois Lullaby.' "

The important thing to keep in mind is that contracts should include musical tasks that require active participation. Let music become engrained in the muscles and sinews of students; stress playing and movement (from swaying to group dances). Point out the relationship between physical tasks and musical concepts. In general, physical involvement will reap greater rewards than purely pencil-and-paper library tasks. This will be discussed further in Chapter 5, in the section on *movement*.

DISCIPLINE

The ability to control people in a classroom situation rates near the top in polls taken of teachers' most frequent and pressing problems. As it holds true for even experienced teachers, so it applies even more to student teachers or first-year teachers. Current writers often urge teachers to break away from rigid control and to permit free movement and discussion to take place in the music room; after all, these writers claim, "music frees us." One may agree or disagree with such statements. Regardless, one point seems obvious: In order for the best kind of learning to take place, the atmosphere must be conducive to such learning. Students need to know the boundaries of acceptable behavior and the purpose of the tasks before them. We know that students come from differing backgrounds and that they learn at varying rates and to various depths. Problems of control stem from many sources, but we shall discuss here only the most frequent and obvious ones.

First, *look to yourself—the teacher—as a source for discipline problems.* Often it is nothing more than your inability to project your voice so that all can hear. Is there variety in your presentation? Do you move at a quick enough pace and get the class caught up in your own enthusiasm? Do you provide daily for some sort of musical success for the students? Do your questions in class defeat the students? Is the language you use effective? Seldom will you find that discipline problems stem from a personal dislike of *you*. Rather, problems often occur as a result of something *YOU* are not doing well.

Second, *are the tasks you assign musically meaningful?* Middle school students are in a stage of rapid physical and social development. Use this to your advantage by presenting students with challenges. For example, instead of asking students "Would any of you like to bow this big bass viol?" present it as a challenge: "Who here is strong enough to hold up this thing?" You will get a better response. Often, students are involved in real or imaginary romances. You could find a pop song about romance and ask students if they can compare it to the *Romeo and Juliet* theme. Would another song have done as well? Why, and why not? This kind of activity solicits the students' views on a matter that deals with sensitivity and expression.

Third, *have you considered all the "nuts-and-bolts" aspects of your lesson?* Under this general heading we place the factors of seating arrangements, location of equipment, and the like. Have you found yourself letting people sit wherever they want? Many times a discipline problem is promoted by the seating arrangement. Some students will "hide" in the back of the room. Perhaps moving them up front would help avoid a problem. If two friends talk together all the time in class, move them away from each other.

Consider, too, the location of the equipment. If you use the piano, it helps to place it at an angle to the class. That way you can play and still observe the class. Avoid playing the piano with your back to the class. If you need to write on the board, see if it could be done before class. If books or other materials are used for every class, plan ahead about how they are to be handed out. You not only waste time passing out things during class, but you may invite discipline problems by losing the pace of activity.

A Checklist of Problems

The following list includes items which are likely to contribute to the problem of discipline.[2] Student teachers would do well to check themselves frequently against this list.

Many observers have noted that:

1. A lesson is often rendered ineffectual because the teacher plunges into the work before getting the attention of each member of the class.
2. The teacher sits at the desk *all* the time, giving the class the cue to settle back indifferently.
3. If a student makes a mistake, the teacher explains the correction directly to him or her instead of to the class as a whole.
4. The teacher does the explaining and answering of questions, instead of encouraging the class to feel a responsibility for all that goes on during the period.
5. The teacher speaks in a low, unconvincing tone which gives the impression that nothing of importance is happening.
6. Students often are seated in straight rows when the tables could easily be arranged in the shape of a horseshoe.

---

2. Adapted from unpublished materials used by Raleigh Schorling, James B. Edmonson, and L.O. Andrews. Used with permission.

7. Teachers allow themselves to be sidetracked by irrelevant questions.
8. Teachers, by their posture and informal attitude, lead students to "take their ease."
9. The teacher is often tied to the textbook, even to a single book.
10. Teachers parrot the students' answers too frequently.
11. Teachers frequently use words and constructions far above the students' comprehension.
12. Both simple and difficult concepts are left before they have been made entirely clear.
13. The wording of questions often is poor.
14. Teachers recite the content for which the students were supposed to be prepared; thus, the interest of the class is lowered.
15. Students are permitted to respond only to the teacher, instead of *discussing* questions with the whole class.
16. Perspective as to importance of materials and activities is often lacking.
17. In assigning work, teachers sometimes say, "I want you to do so and so for me tomorrow." Try to develop a "we" feeling.
18. The lesson is sometimes ended in a sarcastic tone: "You didn't study your lesson well." "Did you have more important things to do?" "I hope next time I teach, you will have a better lesson."
19. Teachers often have little to contribute for the purposes of illustration and stimulation.
20. Statements of pupils are replied to by a monotonous "all right."
21. Teachers talk too rapidly or too slowly. This practice gives the impression that the teacher is nervous, and the slower pupils are unable to follow the train of thought.
22. Too much is given to teaching and too little to learning.
23. Teachers call on a particular student before stating the question.
24. Many teachers fail to write legibly.

Questions & Activities

1. Draw up a sample contract for use in general music, selecting any musical area or skill you wish.
2. If possible, observe a local school in which contracts are used. Discuss with the teacher the rationale for using them; their relative success; the

reactions of students who use this approach. Bring back to class a sample contract to examine its wording and design.

3. Review the benefits and drawbacks of the whole-group, small-group, and individualized classroom arrangements. Suggest activities *other than those listed in the chapter* which would best be handled in (a) the whole-group, (b) the small-group, or (c) the individualized arrangement.

Suggested Readings

Hughes, William, and Kjelson, Lee. *General Music: A Comprehensive Approach, Zone 4*. Menlo Park, Calif.: Addison-Wesley Publishing Company, 1975. See p. xiii.

Monsour, Sally. *Music in Open Education*. New York: The Center for Applied Research in Education, 1974. See pp. 45–53.

National Commission on Instruction. *Individualized Instruction in Music*, compiled by Eunice Boardman Meske and Carroll Rinehart. Reston, Va.: Music Educators National Conference, 1975. See pp. 42–43, 90–93.

Poetter, Jean. "Contracts." *Music Educators Journal* 61, no. 6 (1975): 47–49.

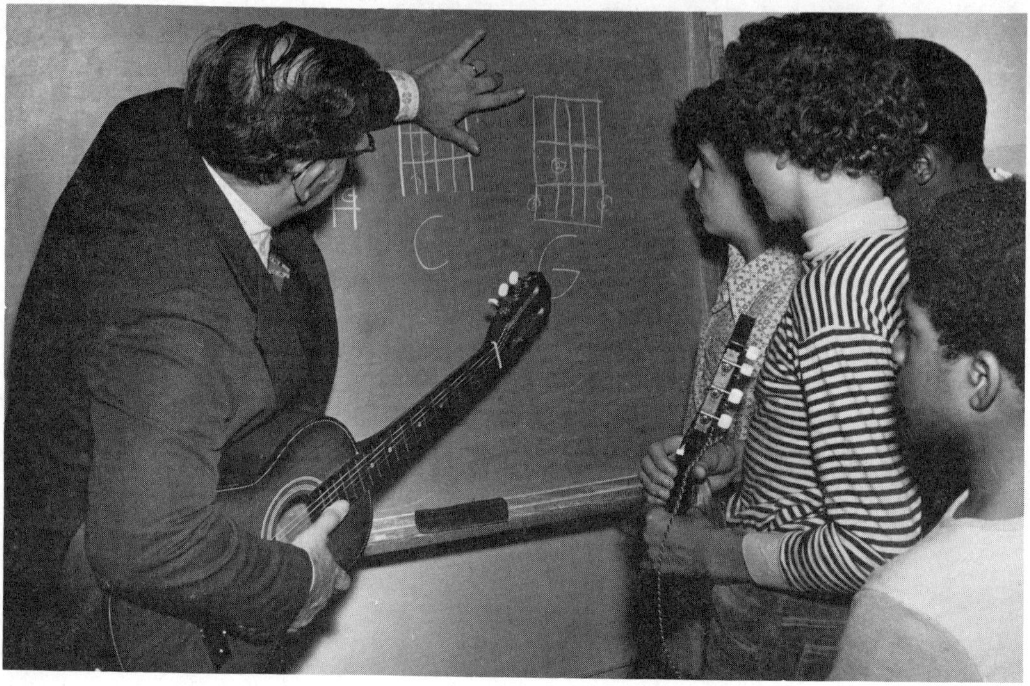
C
G

The chief objection to playing wind instruments is that it prolongs the life of the player.

George Bernard Shaw

Instruments and Materials 4

This chapter is intended to suggest the broad range of possibilities available for making music with classroom instruments. Many music teachers use instruments only occasionally, as "ornament" to singing. But instruments have a great deal to offer in the music class. Students who are too self-conscious to sing, even in a group, may be more responsive when allowed to play simple instruments. The instruments to be discussed are those you will either inherit or purchase to include in your course work. New teachers who want to do more with these musical tools than is touched on here should consult Hood and other sources that deal with them with more depth.[1]

Also consider using any band or orchestra instruments that you own or could borrow from others. If you own an English horn or can borrow a baritone horn, use them in class. Seeing and hearing instruments being played—even if the performance itself is less than ideal—generally has more impact than all the records you might use. Incidentally, if you discuss the instruments (for tone color, perhaps), recruit students from the class, band,

---

1. Marguerite V. Hood, *Teaching Rhythm and Using Classroom Instruments* (Englewood Cliffs, N.J.: Prentice-Hall, Inc., 1970).

or orchestra to come in for a few minutes and demonstrate. Peer recognition can be valuable as you work to develop good attitudes toward music.

BASIC CLASSROOM INSTRUMENTS

Piano

This is probably the instrument most available to you. Most music rooms will have one, though not necessarily in good repair and in tune. You would do yourself a favor—and save time and money later on—to consult with piano tuners about proper piano care, costs for repair of hammers, and so forth.

In addition to accompanying songs in class and performing themes and solo piano works for listening, you can use the piano when dealing with the following:

1. *melody:* comparing the theme as it is played in high, middle, and low registers
2. *intervals*: how they sound and look
3. *scales*: to demonstrate formulas for scale construction. One of the simplest to see and play is the pentatonic, using just the black keys.
4. *harmony*: Notes played as groups can be easily reproduced by students.
5. *tone color*: Experiment with the insides of the piano to see what sorts of sounds it can produce. A good follow-up to this would be Cowell's *Banshee*, and music for prepared piano by Cage.
6. *acoustics*: By silently depressing a chord with the right hand and hitting the fundamental in the lower register, the class can hear the upper strings of the held chord vibrate. This can be done as part of a demonstration of string vibration. Use the bass viol, as its large string size enables the eye to see the vibration. Lay the bass on its back and place V-shaped paper pieces on the low string. As the string is bowed, the pieces should bounce around until they land on the node points and stop bouncing. Harmonics naturally follow as a discussion point.
7. *percussion*: Add the piano to a percussion exercise, using it for tone clusters, "elbow" chords, and so on.

Autoharp

The autoharp is used more frequently in elementary school. However, it can accompany songs and provide harmonic accompaniment to activities in the middle school music class. Most schools have a twelve-bar autoharp (other larger or smaller autoharps are available), and students will play it willingly. The teacher need not be too concerned about *how* students strum it. One can press the chording bars with the right hand and strum with the left, avoiding the crossing-over style favored in the lower grades. Experiment with different picks to alter the tone quality. Make sure the bars are pressed down firmly. Otherwise, a muffled, nonresonant sound will result. Some students enjoy tuning the autoharp at home over a weekend (supply a pitch pipe and instructions).

Use the autoharp for chording songs. Note how chord symbols (G, F^7, B$^\flat$, etc.) in songs tell the player when to change chords. If remedial students are in your class, you may wish to make up a few charts of songs, substituting *colors* for chord symbols. Tape can be placed over the bars and colored with felt-tip markers. In this manner, some who find colors easier to follow than C G // C G // could read this:

$\frac{4}{4}$ (RED)(BLUE)(BLUE)(BLUE) (RED)(BLUE)(BLUE)(BLUE)

Colors can be used in like manner on the piano or fretted instruments.

Percussion

Here we include a huge assortment of drums, sticks, triangle, tambourine, castanets, and so forth. Percussion instruments come in all shapes and sizes. Consider using them all, whenever appropriate. Be selective, or encourage students to choose which of the available instruments would best accompany a song or would retain clarity for a percussion ensemble. Always test students' choices. Often, percussion time becomes chaos time.

In addition to providing a rhythmic background to something else, percussion can be used in the following ways:

1. All percussion plays just the beat.
2. All percussion plays just the melodic rhythm.
3. Drums play on the beat only.
4. Lower-pitched percussion plays every other measure.

The idea is to avoid the random clanging and banging that often occurs in percussion work.

Focus the students' attention on the unique sounds of each instrument. Show correct techniques if students don't know how to play a particular instrument. Note how nonpitched percussion is usually notated in music scores. Avoid complex rhythms and awkward patterns; let the nature and sound of the instrument dictate which should play what:

Basic Classroom Instruments

Many music classes are stocked with homemade "instruments"—coffee cans with gravel inside, hubcaps struck with metal rods, washboards, and so on. These are clearly not in league with a Stradivarius, but they constitute a bridge between school and home. No matter how crude some of these homemade items may be, *never* chide a student for his or her lack of craftsmanship. A student who cares enough to spend personal time making something for music class is a motivated student. Encourage such a student to continue his or her efforts.

Do take notice of the ways in which common percussion instruments can be played. While students ought to learn the traditional approaches of scraping, strumming, and striking such instruments, plan whenever possible to challenge their creativity. Once a song accompaniment or purely percussive passage has been performed adequately, ask the students to invent *different* ways of producing sounds on their instruments. Perhaps a challenge of this type would be appropriate: "I'll give you three minutes to figure out five different ways to make a sound on those instruments. Be ready to perform for the rest of the class." Even if you do not get five suggestions from everyone, there will be enough variations for additional work. Using a bow on the outer edge of a suspended cymbal, using eraser-topped pencils as drumsticks, and rolling the palm of the hand along the loose metal "jingles" of the tambourine are only a few of the many possibilities.

"Now, on scratch paper, figure out a way to notate without words each method of playing." Do not give too many ideas because they may simply copy them, but suggest marks like ↑   ⁀   ↙ ⌐ for the instructions to (*a*) strum upward; (*b*) produce a short, brittle sound; and (*c*) build to crescendo. After students have devised some unique ways and invented notation, review how the sounds can be done piano, forte, with accents, with crescendo, and so on. This, in short, is the main idea behind the spiral approach in music teaching: Return over and over to familiar concepts or materials, and add new applications of techniques and skills.

Tuned Bar Instruments

Under this heading we can include xylophone, marimba, melody bells, song bells, orchestra bells, glockenspiel, metallophone, step bells, sonant bars, resonator bells, and tone bars. Here we examine instruments whose sound is produced by striking wooden or metal bars arranged horizontally or vertically. Some have bars permanently affixed to a framework; some have bars permanently attached to wooden resonator boxes; others have a series of metal bars (Orff), each of which is detachable. Such instruments have great value for work on melody and harmony, among other uses. As with every other type of instrument, you cannot assume that all students know about proper care, handling, and playing. Many students strike the bar with a mallet and let the mallet head remain down, preventing vibration. Using two mallets at the same time may be hard for some students.

Melodic ostinati are good introductions to the instruments. Pentatonic improvisations (with the fourth and seventh tones removed) should be familiar to some. Different types of mallets can be experimented with for unusual sounds. A randomly arranged chromatic series of tone bars can reinforce tone-row music. Tone bars can be grouped into triads for work in harmony. Colored tape (or numbers or something else) can be affixed to instruments for those students needing remedial work.

Guitar

The importance of the guitar in music classes has received much attention. Although the piano is still the most essential classroom instrument, the guitar has been accepted more and more in music classes at every grade. The influence of pop/rock music in music education likely has stirred the interest in guitars (electric and acoustic) more than any logical need. Certainly, guitars are more portable than piano and more challenging than autoharp. It cannot be assumed, however, that the guitar has replaced—or will replace—the piano. Keyboard instruments are more adaptable to the needs of the general music class. Among other features, the size of keyboard instruments permits more than one player at a time. Songs in series books have varied accompaniments for keyboard, while not all songs are arranged for simplified guitar performance.

Unless the teacher is gifted on fretted instruments (possible, but uncommon), his or her use of the guitar probably will be limited to strumming simple accompaniments to songs. But even an ability to chord a song using I, IV, and V^7 would be valuable musically and socially in the classroom. Most students are used to hearing guitar music through records and TV, though it is usually produced by electric instruments. Some students will show interest in folk guitar because they like Judy Collins or Joan Baez. Few students have any knowledge of classical guitar styles (for example, Segovia). Perhaps the classical area is one you might want to expose your classes to, especially if you yourself can play in that style.

The attraction of guitar goes beyond listening appreciation. *Strumming* a guitar appeals to the sense of touch. Some middle schools have enough money to fund the purchase of twenty to thirty guitars so that whole-class instruction may take place. Countless beginning guitar courses have been published, complete with wall charts, slides, film strips, tapes, and records. Students can learn basic fingerings for chords and strum along with pop hits (most pop sheet music includes guitar symbols). One caution: If you have students playing the guitar in class, either as a group or singly, remember one of the cardinal rules—*plan for relatively easy and quick success.* Steel strings are difficult to press down for chording; unless calluses have been built up, some students will have pain. When that happens regularly, the fun and enjoyment suffer and students may not volunteer anymore for guitar playing. Here are two simple techniques that might help both the students and the progress of your lesson:

1. *Buy gut strings.* For a few dollars you can purchase a complete set of six classical guitar strings. They may be clear gut or silver-wound strings. Either way, they are much easier to chord and strum than steel strings. Experiment with different picks to alter the tone color.

2. *Employ scordatura.* Eliminate the problem of awkward fingering by tuning the guitar to a major chord. Without increasing the tension of the strings, you can tune the guitar down to a C major or D major chord, as shown here:

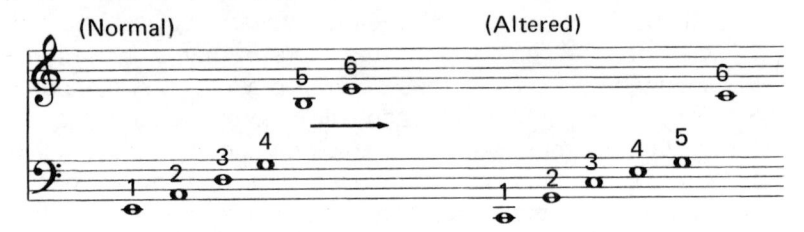

Students can then easily play I, IV, and V by sliding one finger up and down across the strings, or by using a pencil or, if you wish, the heavier, smooth metal bar used for Hawaiian guitar playing. In any case, students will be able to play along with a minimum of effort.

Handbells

Special mention should be made about handbells. Unlike the extremely inexpensive plastic slide whistles, handbells are costly. Few companies make them, and their proper care and handling are important. Nevertheless, you should consider handbells for your classes (see Appendix C for where to write). Unlike whistles and ocarinas, handbells have an interesting history, and there is an extensive literature.

The use of handbells has been limited primarily to church and

Instruments and Materials   43

occasionally music educators' conventions. However, handbells are desirable for classroom use because they:

1. have a beautiful sound
2. are easily managed by students in grades 6 to 9
3. appeal to the sense of touch
4. can be used to perform a wide range of music
5. can be shared among groups of performers
6. can serve in the same way as tone bars in lessons dealing with harmony
7. can be the basis for the forming of a performance ensemble
8. demand individual contributions for the good of the group

Handbells were developed to serve as a warm-up or rehearsal before pulling steeple bells. Teachers who plan to use handbells in class would do well to study the history of bell ringing and the complex art of change ringing.

The great amount of skill involved in English bell ringing is truly inspiring. However, our needs are really far less demanding. Handbells, in sets of fifteen bells or more, are a joy to play and easy to teach. Even students who can't read notes can do well in a bell choir. The best bell choirs do have screening tests to examine note-reading ability and wrist and arm strength. But your students can learn to play in a few minutes. The following approach is one that should work with students who do not read notes.

Suppose you have a chromatic set of twenty-five bells (two octaves) which ring from G below middle C to high G atop the treble clef. Suppose further that ten non-music-reading students have expressed interest in learning to play bells. Consider translating the musical work into *numbers* first. This will be much easier for such students to follow and will allow the musical selection to be heard quickly. We'll take the final phrase of the traditional Protestant Doxology (*Old Hundredth*) to clarify how the approach might work.

1. First, number each bell on paper as follows:

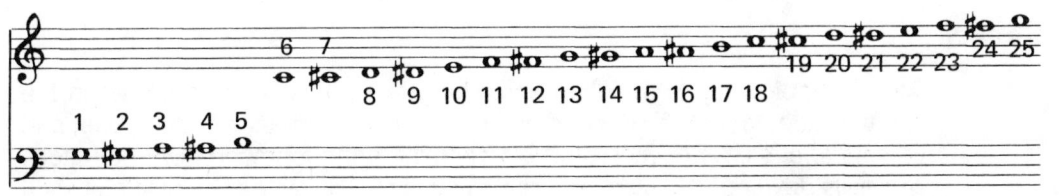

2. Next, consider the overall range of the selected piece, with particular attention to bass and melodic lines.

3. Trace a numerical sketch of the harmonic/melodic motion, using the numbers above for each note in the original. Thus:

Old Hundred—ending

```
20 | 17   13   15   18  | 17   15   13  ⌒||
 8 |  8   10   12  10-12|  13   12    8   ||
 5 |  5    5    8    8  |   8   8-6   5   ||
 1 |  1    1    3    3  |  5-6   𝄽    1  ⌣||
```

4. Check to see that as many essential harmonic tones are included as can be. Rather than reduce the scheme, try to include as many bells and players as common sense dictates.

5. Develop your own notation. For nonreaders, you need not use 𝄽 or ━●━, and you may simplify with ━ ━ for two beats of rest.

6. Rewrite the whole piece using numbers 1–25. As often as possible, keep a continuing bass, especially in hymn-like pieces.

7. When completed, check to see how many separate bells will be needed to perform the piece. To keep it simple at first, have each person play one bell (and be responsible for one number). Over time, each player can be assigned two or more bells.

8. To help control attention and eye focus, get a large, white poster board from the local bookstore. Arrange your numbered musical score on it using large numbers drawn with a thick felt-tipped marker. That way, you can have one master score to point to as all follow and play.

9. In time, break away from this kind of notation to the standard kind. All bell-choir music is printed using the regular clefs, notes, and rests, though color is used occasionally.

With proper care and polishing, handbells can add a unique ingredient to the music class. Feel free to (*a*) arrange pop songs for bells, (*b*) add them into your next choir concert, (*c*) use them as triadic arrangements for harmony lessons, and (*d*) accompany class songs with bells.

Recorder

Most school systems maintain something like a flutophone program in the fourth grade, for a dual purpose: to help teach note reading to everyone, and to help spot students interested in becoming band members. Unfortunately, the skills developed in such programs usually fall away, and most fifth or sixth graders never pick up the instrument again. Thus, many middle school students will have had some experience on these simple tone producers. You can make the most of these unused abilities.

The recorder is centuries old. As a result, a vast amount of printed recorder music is available. Recorders come in a range of styles, models, and costs. Professionals usually favor the expensive pearwood models, but your choice should be based on practicality and low cost. By all means, choose a plastic model, with a right-hand thumb hook or rest. Examine the many recorder methods books and select one with a variety of good melodies (not nursery school level), folk songs, and ensemble arrangements. Consider taking enough money from the music budget to buy recorders for each member of your largest class to use. Shop around the local instrument stores and obtain bids. Try out all the available models yourself. Do not mix models; you will find differences in sound. Look for models that have a movable lower section—a feature that (*a*) permits more accurate tuning and (*b*) allows students to adapt their instruments to the shape of their right hand.

If you do add the recorder into the music program, be aware that not every student will take to the opportunity with enthusiasm. But recorders, as with all classroom instruments, appeal first to one's sense of touch. Many students who refuse to sing in class will try to play the recorder; such an instrument seems to require a less personal effort than singing. Enlist students who have had some recorder or recorder-like experience to help the beginners.

Approach the recorder as you do the autoharp or piano—not as a rigidly enforced, unchangeable class routine but as one chance for musical experience. Recorders need not be regarded as merely solo instruments. They can be used for descants to familiar songs and for harmonic ensemble work. Stress good tone production (students always overblow), ensemble discipline, and proper care of the instrument. Unless soap and hot water are handy, consider buying a jar of germicidal mouthpiece dip from an instrument store. With it, you can safely use the instruments class after class.

If you are lucky enough to develop a small group of recorder fans, you can form a recorder club. Check into the cost of buying instruments other than the soprano recorder. Feed the interest of club members by playing recordings of groups such as the Krainis Consort. Try to schedule brief public appearances for your club—at assemblies, local libraries, and concerts. Above all, encourage each member as much as possible.

Other Instruments

Before leaving our discussion of classroom instruments, let us note some other music-producing instruments that are not always considered. The humble *harmonica*, *slide whistle*, *ocarina*, and *ukulele* all can be used. Some students may already show ability on such instruments. Providing the opportunity to use this talent in class could strongly motivate these students. Show your own interest by going to the local music store and trying each of these instruments. Ask about cost and durability. Play them yourself. See if you can get brochures that describe their price range and how they are made. Harmonicas, for example, cost from $2 to over $100. As long as the use of these instruments is enjoyable and purposeful, add any or all of them.

CLASSROOM MATERIALS

Record-Playing System

Most music classrooms do have a record player, but too many teachers know very little about its proper use and maintenance. Before you actually use this machine, acquaint yourself with the knobs and dials that control the operation. Locate the on–off switch for the turntable; the on–off switch for the amplifier; the boost knobs for treble, bass, and stereo balance. Some machines have a built-in device for checking the accuracy of the turntable speed. Of course, the needle should be checked regularly for wear. Inspect the back of the record player to find the placement of speaker jacks, the microphone plug socket, and such. If the record player is to be a permanent piece of equipment in the classroom, it would be wise to get the speakers mounted on the walls. That way, the sound is carried better and you avoid the problem of tripping over yards of wire.

Records

Records should be stored vertically and in their jackets. Keep the record grooves clean by wiping occasionally with an inexpensive, store-bought chemically treated cloth or a slightly damp, lint-free rag. Records should be kept away from heat (radiators, strong sunlight) and away from chalk dust.
For locating parts of selections within non-banded discs, the following hints may be helpful. Some record players have a built-in scale gauge which projects out over the turntable. You need only (a) remember the number on that scale where a portion—say, the development section—occurs; (b) move the tone arm to that number; and (c) lower the needle. Most players will *not* have this gadget, so a piece of cardboard (more durable than paper) can be used. Cut a strip about one inch wide and long enough to fit from the center hole to beyond the outer edge of the record. Punch a hole in one end of this strip and place the strip over the spindle. When the tone arm moves to the portion (such as the development section) that you wish to be able to locate exactly in the future, place a small mark or dot on the strip in line with the location of the needle at that point. You can continue to mark such portions throughout the entire side. When this is completed, title the cardboard strip with name of the piece, composer, record label name, and performance group. (Another version of the same work, differing in tempo and interpretation, will reduce the effectiveness of the cardboard strip.)

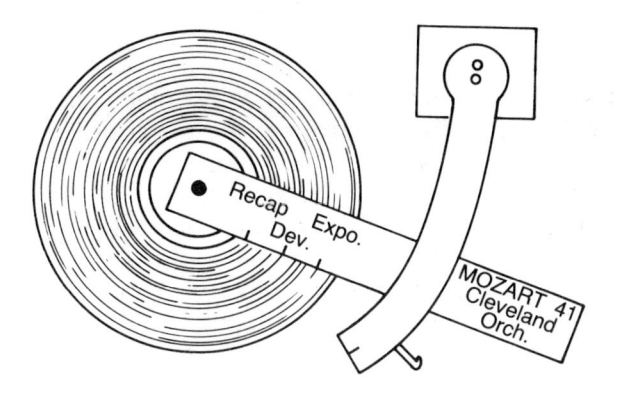

Tape Recorders

More and more, music teachers are recognizing the value of using tape and tape machines in class. Following are some specific uses that have proven to be practical and creative.

1. Prerecording musical examples from records allows for more efficient use of time in class work. Motives, passages, sections, or whole works can be taped ahead of time. Using tape avoids fumbling with misplaced records, uneven turntable speeds, and dull needles. Further, finding specific portions is fast and accurate through the use of the built-in counter.
2. Taping various musical activities in class—for example, rhythmic work, songs, and improvisations—gives students the opportunity to listen to their efforts and to make critical judgments.
3. Taping several parts of a three- or four-voice round in smaller classes can free the class to concentrate on fewer voice parts. In like manner, songs with instrumental obbligati can be performed by recording the whole class performing one part and then, on the playback, having them play the other part.
4. Simple experiments with feedback, and correlating speed and pitch, can be done with most reel-to-reel machines.
5. Tape loops and musical experiments with tape can be both fun and instructive. Students can create and record an ostinato to a given song on a tape loop. As it is played back, the whole class can sing and accompany themselves at the same time.

For further information, teachers should consult series texts and publications dealing with the operation and use of tape machines in music class.[2]

---

2. See, for example, Mary V. Marsh, Carroll A. Rinehart, and Edith J. Savage, "Electronic Music," *The Spectrum of Music* (New York: Macmillan, 1975).

Textbooks

Just about every middle school has adopted some music series book (e.g., Silver Burdett). These books are the result of years of planning and hard work by many qualified writers and editors. Use songs from one book, activities from another, recordings from yet another. Series textbooks can be used as a guide, but the teacher often needs to change and select according to the needs of the class.

Someday, you might be a member of a committee which examines and evaluates new textbooks. Here are some areas of concern to keep in mind:

1. overall musical quality of the contents
2. quality, quantity, and appropriateness of the song literature
3. quality of the photography and of the color in art reproductions
4. strength and quality of the binding (many of the plastic-comb bindings will crack; metal spiral binders may scratch the piano)
5. weight of the paper (too thin?)
6. quality of the recordings that can be purchased to accompany the text
7. the presence/absence of suggested lesson plans and supplemental work
8. cost
9. availability of worksheets and overhead projectuals (supplemental)
10. presence/absence of *sequence* in material (i.e., does it progress in an orderly and step-by-step way?)
11. correspondence (note page numbers) between student edition and teacher edition.

Media

Mention already has been made about record-playing systems and tape recorders. However, the media resources available in most school systems are vast. It is suggested that every would-be music teacher take a media workshop sometime during the college years. Knowing how to operate the various types of photocopying machines can lessen the burden of the classroom teacher. Further, a knowledge of copyright restrictions is vital.

Video equipment is available in larger school systems. Slide projectors with carousels and 8 mm–16 mm film projectors generally can be found. Unless your school system is large enough to sponsor clubs such as a film club or amateur projectionists, you will have to order, sign out, operate, and return all such equipment. If a workshop on media is not offered at your college, visit the media center. You will be amazed at how quickly you can gain the knowledge necessary for you to feel confident in using school equipment.

Special mention should be made here of two similar pieces of equipment: the *opaque* and the *overhead* projectors. The opaque projector is of much older design. It is a large, bulky machine that projects upon a wall or screen (in a darkened room) the magnified image of large items—pages of a book, 8 × 10 photos, and the like. If you want to show a complete page from an essay or a full-page musical composition on staff paper, you do so with this machine. Its size need not put you off; if you plan to have students write music in class and discuss their efforts, this machine can be most helpful. As with any projector, it makes the class focus its attention. Seat work can be taken and projected immediately—a great time-saver. One word of caution: The projector bulb is high in wattage, and therefore very hot. Be careful to avoid prolonged showing of any item. The heat can warp page edges or damage photos.

The overhead projector is probably more familiar to most readers. It is less bulky than the opaque, but it does require a certain amount of space (usually on a portable cart with wheels). It projects an image over and behind the operator. With an adjustable device, this machine can be used at varying distances from the wall or screen. The image to be projected must be transferred to a transparent acetate sheet; one can use felt-tipped markers or crayons or china markers. The overhead projector can be used to project song lyrics, notation of musical themes, student work, and multicolored transparencies (to name only a few uses).

This machine is ideal for rooms with small chalkboards. As with the opaque projector, it helps focus the attention of a class. Because you *face* the class as you operate it (the class sees the magnified image behind you), you can watch the students and point or spotlight items as you go along. Further, listening charts or historical time lines can be prepared, used, and saved. In like manner, outstanding student effort—say, in composition—can be preserved on clear acetate (available in any office equipment store).

The overhead projector also takes a continuous acetate roll which can be turned or rotated for special projections. One could use this in a longer listening scheme in which "attention arrows" are drawn from one part to another. Or use this roll of acetate for an improvisatory exercise in which students respond musically to cues given from an ever-moving roll of instructions. Colors, too, can be used for spotlighting.

These two types of projectors were suggested here not because they are the *best* equipment to have, or because the music teacher cannot do without them. However, the music teacher faces special problems and has unique needs. On a day-to-day-basis, such projectors could well receive more use than all the types of film and video machinery put together. But even the finest equipment will not redeem a lesson that is failing because of poor planning and lack of variety. On the other hand, good lessons can be made even better through wise use of media. Learn the operation of as many pieces of equipment as you can; consult with teachers of English, math, and social studies to find out how they use such equipment.

Questions & Activities

1. Select any of the classroom instruments mentioned and prepare a list of as many possible musical uses for it as you can. Be imaginative but practical. Share your list with the rest of the class.
2. Prepare tape loops of rhythmic or melodic ostinati. Turn these into a brief lesson on rhythm work, or use them for song accompaniment.
3. Select any song—e.g., from a series book, a folk song, or a popular ballad—and arrange an instrumental accompaniment using some combination of autoharp, tuned bar instruments, recorders, and/or something else. Write out the arrangement, using any scheme of notation that seems easy to read and understand.
4. Ask your school/university representative to visit your class to discuss the care, use, and purchase of educational hardware. Look into the possibility of visiting a local school that is scheduling a media workshop.
5. Make a list of the ways the following pieces of equipment may be used—traditionally or inventively—in the general music class:
    a. slide projector
    b. 8mm or 16mm film projector
    c. overhead projector
    d. opaque projector
    e. tape recorder

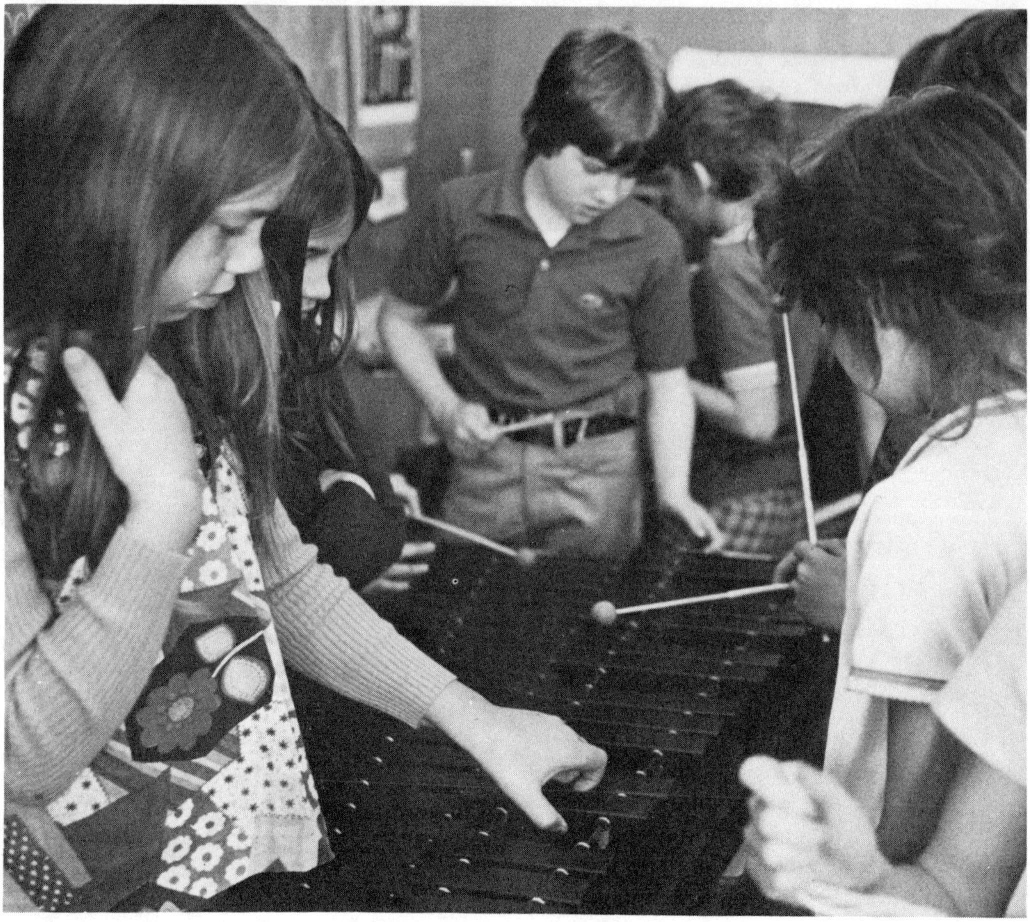

The best form of musical appreciation is to try and do it for yourself: to get really inside the meaning of music.

Ralph Vaughan Williams

Classroom Activities 5

Throughout the history of American music instruction, singing has played a central role. *The Bay Psalm Book*, the first book printed in the United States (in 1640), was a collection of texts to be sung. During the next two centuries, vocal music was considered the only worthwhile variety of music. It is understandable, therefore, that when music instruction was introduced in Boston schools in 1838, it was *vocal* music, not instrumental. To this day, when we think of a typical music class we still presume it to be singing-oriented.

SINGING

Singing, long considered the *only* activity or at least the most important, has come to be thought of differently in recent years. Singing should indeed remain an important part of a well-rounded general music program. One need not be a singer to appreciate and understand how music works. However, for many students singing seems to be a natural, easy musical activity.

Singing, more than performing instrumental music, is a very personal matter. Some students recoil from the idea of singing, not because they can't sing but because they fear not measuring up to peer expectations. If a teacher chides such students, he or she many lose them forever. Thus, although singing should continue as an activity, some students will not take part easily or willingly. The wise teacher will explore other avenues to musical involvement (simple instrumental ostinati, improvising drum rhythms, tasks such as "textbook monitor" or "chairman of the record player," and the like).

The singing voice of students in the middle school grades is a curious thing. Such voices are less childlike than fifth grade chorus, yet not as mature as the high school a cappella choir. For the most part, vocal problems at this level are male, not female. Generally, the difference between an eighth-grade female soprano and an alto is only a few notes in range; perhaps a slightly heavier, darker color characterizes the alto. But for general purposes, all girls can sing the same lines. Boys, however, are different in this regard.

The "care and feeding" of the adolescent male voice has been the subject of a considerable amount of research and opinion. Some teachers think boys should continue to sing, but quietly, throughout the voice "change"—that normal process of maturing in which vocal cords lengthen and thicken. Some English choirmasters suggest no singing at all until the change seems completed. Some advise boys not to yell or shout in athletic activity; others say it will not hurt a bit. If the experts cannot agree, what is a teacher to do with boys' voices? Are there any broad guidelines that might help?

Obviously, the music teacher must realize that male voices begin to change during adolescence. Some voices seem to change overnight (or over summer vacation), while others change gradually. This change can begin in elementary school or not until ninth grade, but changes *will* occur that are detectible. *Be on the lookout for changes you can see or hear* (facial hair, more mature bone structure, lower speaking voice, etc.) When these changes occur, you must be willing and able to adjust the vocal demands placed upon the boys. Why is this so important?

Cooper and Kuersteiner concluded that many boys do not get involved in singing because the *range* of songs is defeating.[1] In a random assortment of adolescent boys and girls, they could combine on a unison song only if the range did not exceed this:

Cooper and Kuersteiner discovered that most song series contained many songs that exceeded this range. Let us examine Cooper and Kuersteiner's ranges:

---

[1]. Irvin Cooper and Karl O. Kuersteiner, *Teaching Junior High School Music*, 2nd ed. (Boston: Allyn & Bacon, 1970).

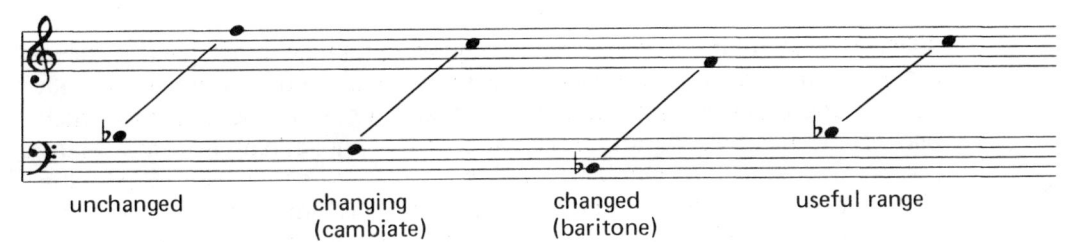

unchanged | changing (cambiate) | changed (baritone) | useful range

Publishers seem to have adopted this idea of usable unison. Songs in *Silver Burdett Music* have a composite range of B–C'; [2] *Sound, Beat, and Feeling* has an average range of C–d'.[3] One publishing company now offers choral music arranged within Cooper and Kuersteiner's range limitations.[4]

What you, as a general music teacher, must bear in mind is that:

1. Boys' voices will change in range and quality.
2. Boys will get involved if the songs you choose don't exceed their physical capacity.
3. The ability to find (or arrange yourself) properly voiced vocal arrangements is necessary for success in teaching middle school music.

How do you know if Bobby Rose is still a soprano? Could he be a cambiata (changing voice), or boy-alto, or alto-tenor? A teacher needs to know methods for voice testing in order to select (and perhaps arrange) music intelligently.

Voice Testing

Probably the oldest approach to testing voices is to call each student forward to sing individually. This creates intense student trauma and nervousness. (Fear alone can cause contraction of every muscle and tendon in the body.) One might well question the value of conclusions drawn from such an approach. It can be argued that the unique quality and range of each voice can be analyzed only individually. But the time spent, combined with the repellent effect on students, may not net the results one seeks in general music. The size of the class, the time available, and the degree to which singing is deemed important are the criteria for selecting this approach to voice testing.

In any method of testing, look for a number of things. Do not be

---

2. Reimer et al., *Silver Burdett Music, Grade 7* (Morristown, N. J.: Silver Burdett, 1975).
3. Robert A. Choate, Barbara Kaplan, and James Standifer, *Sound, Beat, and Feeling, Grade 7* (New York: American Book Company, 1976).
4. Cambiata Press, P. O. Box 1151, Conway, Arkansas 72032.

satisfied with range alone; listen for quality. Though most girls in these grades have similar overall ranges, listen for that ideal register when both volume and ease of tone production prevail. Check (*a*) the ability to match pitch, (*b*) reading ability, and (*c*) capacity to distinguish high from low. Many teachers place all girls who can read notation in the alto section. But let the girls switch between alto and soprano. You will find that most girls will automatically sing the melody of a song unless you specify a certain group for a harmony line. There is little damage done if a "soprano" is asked to join the alto ranks. There are few "true" altos in middle school.

For your voice examination, consider the following:

1. general warm-up (on an open vowel), perhaps

    and modulate
2. scale drill—Start on middle C (for girls) and modulate upward.
3. tone matching—Strike isolated notes on the piano and have students sing back as quickly as possible.
4. reading—Provide easy patterns, perhaps with one or two accidentals to check reading.
5. songs—Turn to familiar songs such as folk songs, Christmas carols, or pop songs. Such a choice helps relax the singer and allows you to hear better the true quality of the voice.

These suggestions are suitable only if you choose to test voices individually. The idea is to proceed as quickly as possible. Remember, your class is not the a cappella choir. Voice testing is done mainly because it affords some insight into the unique aspects of every music class and it aids the teacher in selecting vocal repertoire.

Find songs that are strong, such as call-and-response songs, chanties, and work chants. Locate songs that permit easy ostinati, both vocally and instrumentally. Many songs have extremely simple harmonic backgrounds. Even today, the familiar I–VI–II–V^7 pattern is found in many vocal works. Most classes will have boys with changing voices and, therefore, limited ranges; consider ostinati as basic as the following for them.

I   VI   II   V   I   VI   II   V

Whole-group testing is far more efficient, although you won't be able to check for subtle differences in voices. Such an approach is quick and it avoids the fear arising from individual tests. Cooper and Kuersteiner have devised a six-step procedure for voice classification: [5]

1. Talk briefly about different voices and the importance of all voice parts for a good choral sound.
2. Have girls sit in the back of the room, with all the boys in the front few rows.
3. Start "Jingle Bells" in D major. All boys are to sing in the register most comfortable for them. As they sing it, move among them and tap on the shoulder all those who are singing in the lower register (baritones). When tapped, each boy should stop singing. When done, have all those "baritones" move to the rear.
4. Remaining singers are either sopranos or cambiate ("changing"). Resume "Jingle Bells," but this time, sing it in A♭ major. Listen for the sopranos, tapping them as you detect them and have them cease singing. Once completed, have the tapped boy-sopranos move back, leaving only the group of cambiate singers.
5. Having identified, however roughly, groups of (a) girls, (b) boy-sopranos, (c) cambiate, and (d) baritones, have the baritones sing "John Brown's Body" in D♭ major to check your classifications. Once convinced of your placement, have the cambiate group do the same song in A♭ major. Make adjustments, if necessary, on the basis of this last check. Then arrange the groups as follows:

GIRLS

Baritones   Boy Sopranos

                  Cambiata

Piano

6. With this arrangement, let everyone sing "John Brown's Body" in D♭ major. While not essential, it allows the girls to participate and provides a concluding experience for this testing procedure.

---

5. Cooper and Kuersteiner, *Teaching Junior High Music*, pp. 30–37.

This short summary of the six-step procedure is suggested only as a guide. If you choose to emphasize singing in your classes, you will want to consult Cooper's written work in detail.

For general purposes, the whole-group approach is far better than individual tests. It is quick, acceptable to students, and reasonably efficient. It highlights the importance of separating male voices. If you wish to avoid accepting all of Cooper and Kuersteiner's steps, simplify them. What you seek basically is to sort out low male voices from those somewhere in the middle (boy-sopranos are easy to locate). These simple group exercises do the job. Use up-to-date, familiar songs. Song ranges should be similar: "Jingle Bells" spans five notes (a, b); "John Brown's Body" spans an octave (c, d). Note, too, the tessitura of the songs you substitute. Use these ranges:

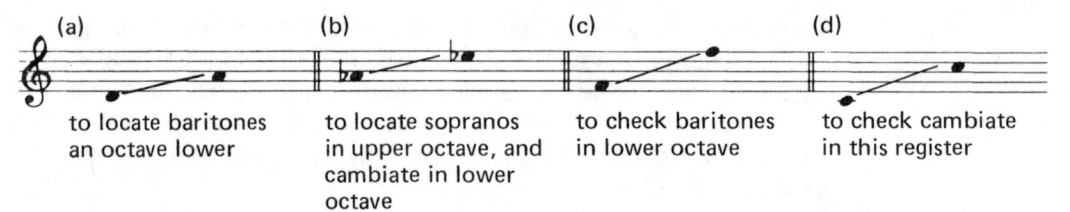

(a)	(b)	(c)	(d)
to locate baritones an octave lower	to locate sopranos in upper octave, and cambiate in lower octave	to check baritones in lower octave	to check cambiate in this register

Once all this has been accomplished, choose your song literature carefully. Songs should permit adding of parts to the unison melody line, and separate parts should be provided for your vocal groups. Here are some further suggestions:

1. Check frequently with your local sheet music dealer. Keep up-to-date with new arrangements. Do not automatically purchase everything marked "S.A.B." (soprano/alto/baritone) just because you may have heard that S.A.B. arrangements are suitable for adolescent choirs. The cambiate group is usually shortchanged (bass line is too low, alto line is too high).

2. Examine many middle-school-level series books, not just the one your school owns. Every series has its own approach, emphasis, and song repertoire.

3. Get in the habit of writing out simple melodic lines, of very limited range, to unison songs the class enjoys. You don't have to be a Stravinsky to make up easy extra parts. Consider the upper and lower limits of the boys in each class, and arrange accordingly. Avoid rapid, intervalic shifts and patterns that do not repeat. The key is *simplicity* without tedium.

4. As with every musical activity, your enthusiasm and positive comments will go a long way in making singing a pleasurable, nonthreatening experience.

READING MUSIC

Music teachers continually face the problem of helping students decipher musical hieroglyphs. Certainly, many elementary schools do an admirable job in trying to develop note-reading skills. However, these skills require constant attention in every grade.

Some middle school students have had almost no work in note reading. They may be reluctant to plunge willingly into singing a new song. What will you use for song material? How important is note reading in your philosophy of music teaching? Is note reading of central or only minor importance?

The most important consideration is the amount of time available to you and your classes. Solid reading skills cannot be developed in half a year in the middle school. Do you wish to devote the greater part of every class to reading skills? Is it reading skills per se you wish to develop, or the experience of music making that results from such reading?

Students learn best when they are confronted with "need-to-know" situations. If students can be shown that an enjoyable musical activity could be even better if they possessed certain skills, the students are likely to become more motivated. Thus, music making should take priority over isolated skill development. There is nothing actually wrong with rote singing. The problem is simply that rote learning fosters dependence rather than independence. Music educators must focus on sharpening the abilities of students so that they may produce and appreciate music enjoyably after they leave the school.

Some students will be able to read standard notation. They will be willing to sing or play, and they will have expectations for success. But others will just sit and watch. They may never have had any success in music class. Low expectations, poor grades, and voice changes make note reading entirely loathsome to some students. For them, the notation might as well be Greek. Your job is to simplify the task, encourage the students, and respond favorably to *any* effort.

Let's take a look at some previous systems to rewrite music so that the novice could meet with success (see Figure 5.1). Some of these notations are more fanciful than others. Tufts's notation added solfege syllables into a staff which shows melodic contour. Harrison's, perhaps the most basic notation, had the advantage of unadorned numerals, but it lacked the support of a clear visual contour. The adaptation of the much earlier English "fasola scheme" (that is, schemes built around the scale progression fa–sol–la–fa–sol–la–mi) is evident.

Perhaps of even greater influence and potential is the scheme known as shape notes (see Figure 5.2). Devised about 1801, shape notes (or "buckwheat" notes) are still with us. One can still buy hymnals printed in

FIGURE 5.1 *Old Hundred*

Source: George Pullen Jackson, *White Spirituals in the Southern Uplands* (Chapel Hill: University of North Carolina Press, 1933), p. 343. Used with permission.

shape notes. Shape notes (with up to seven different shapes) are placed upon a standard staff in the usual way. The strength of the system lies in the fact that while the melodic contour is always apparent, the various shapes indicate the function of each tone in the melodic sequence. Children trained to read music with shape notes have been shown to be more accurate in their sight reading.[6] One can experience the use of shape notes by observing and hearing a performance at the Sacred Harp singing days still held in the South. The history of the development and use of shape notes is indeed interesting; it is mentioned here because many children—especially those of Appalachian/Southern background—are quite familiar with this type of notation. If for nothing more than its historic value, do look into shape note notation—an aspect of our music history that is just as American as jazz.

---

6. George Kyme, "An Experiment in Teaching Children to Read Music with Shape Notes," *Journal of Research in Music Education* 8, no. 1 (Spring 1960): 3–8.

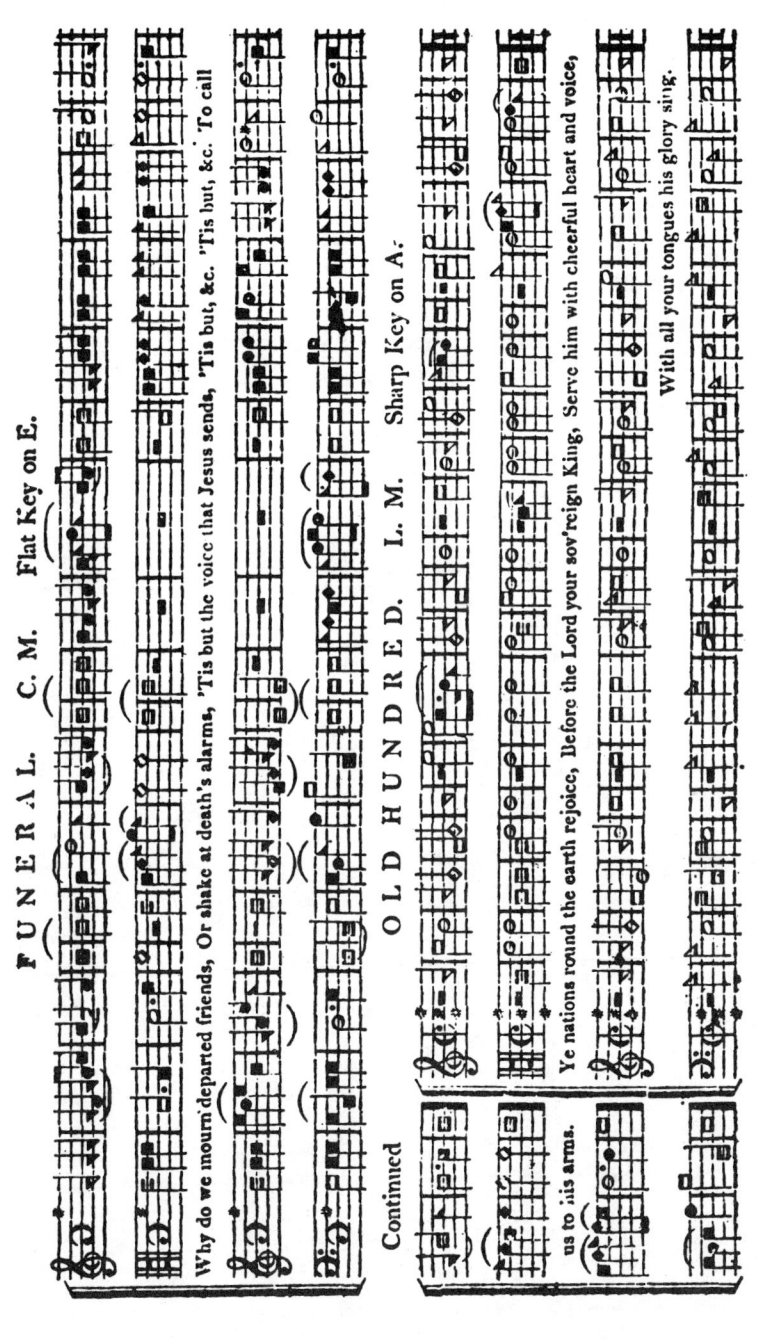

FIGURE 5.2 *A Page From The Oldest Known Shape-Note Book*

Source: George Pullen Jackson, *White Spirituals in the Southern Uplands* (Chapel Hill: University of North Carolina Press, 1933), p. 2. Used with permission.

62 Reading Music

If your students have a pretty good grasp of standard notation, you should not resort to less sophisticated forms of notation. But if reading notation is a struggle, and if musical progress seems to suffer because of this difficulty, feel free to use any visual scheme that encourages *positive, relatively quick* musical results. It is much easier to introduce standard notation to students who want to learn it because they feel secure and have been successful in earlier reading activities. In other words, success breeds motivation, and motivated learners learn more quickly and easily.

If your classes need remedial work and fail to respond to shape notes or numbers, try to move gradually from very simple symbols to more complex ones. Consider the song "America" approached in this manner (see Figure 5.3).

The whole idea is to make the reading of symbols easy and musically productive. Use colors if you wish. But make it so simple that you can produce a musical result quickly. Gradually you can move away from fanciful designs toward the kind of notation (standard) that students will inevitably encounter later in life. Stress direction, contour, and movement in

FIGURE 5.3 *America*

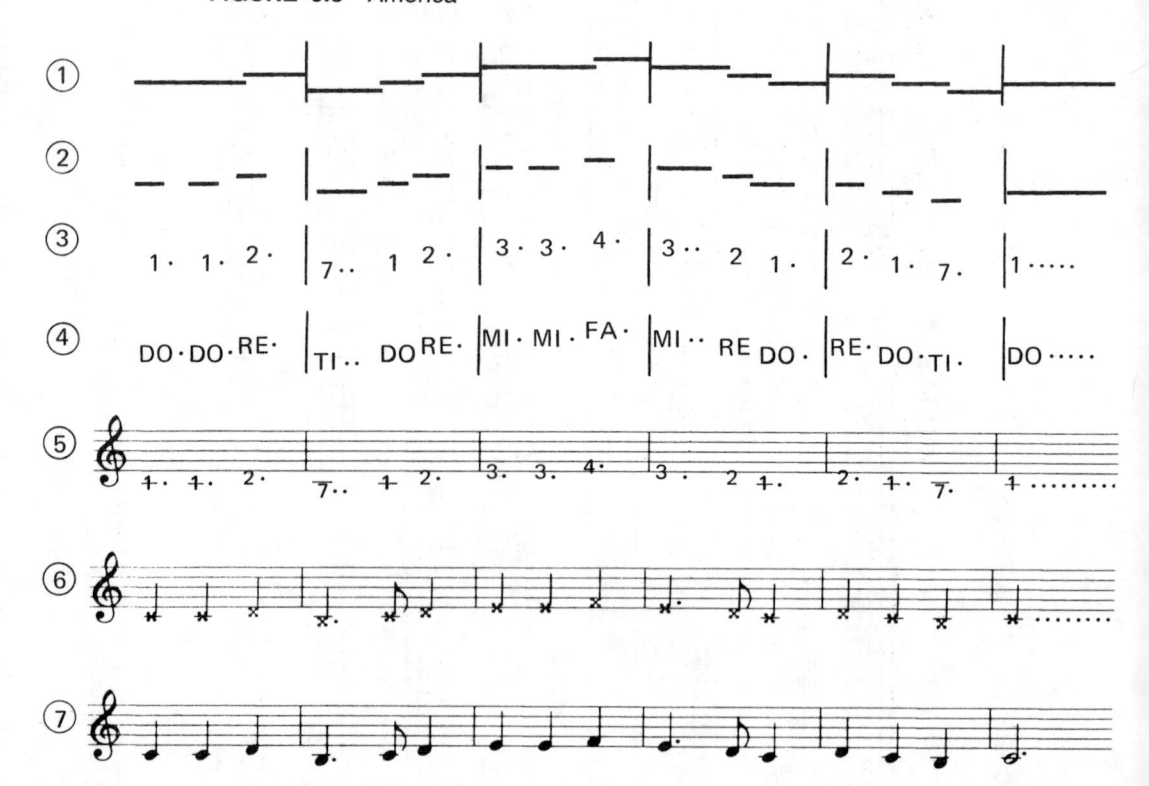

FIGURE 5.4

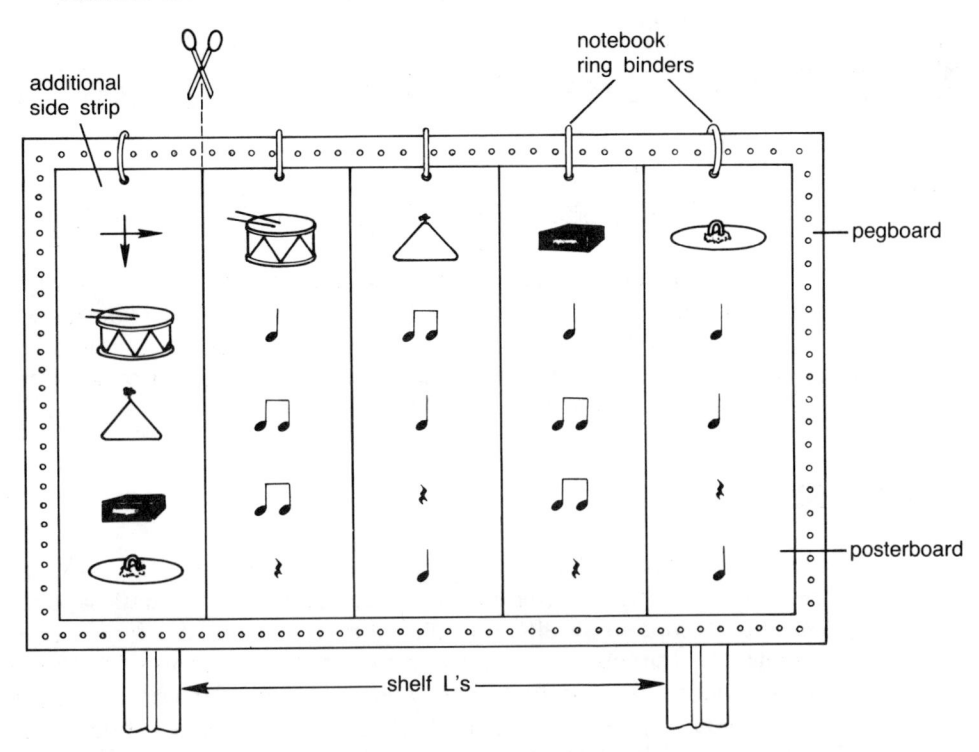

A visual aid for rhythmic reading that can be constructed in an evening. It uses only a large sheet of pegboard, two L's for supporting shelves, some nuts and bolts, and four or five separate ring binders. Poster board can be used, cut into four equal vertical strips. One could start with easy rhythm patterns and gradually increase the difficulty. As each vertical strip is one beat, you can devise your own scheme of repetition and novelty. The strip on the far left indicates the classroom instrument that is to play each line. You could cover this strip and use the arrangement shown in the top horizontal strip (with each instrument playing only a certain beat in each measure). Additional blank vertical strips could cover the first or last beat and turn the drill into 3/4 meter. This aid frees the teacher from extra chalkboard work and also points to the variety of student ability. If read vertically, the drummer could stay on simple patterns; by turning over several strips, the woodblock player could try a more challenging level.

melodic lines. Trace contours with chalk or with your hand. Ask students to graph a well-known melody and check the results. Better still, let students learn the "how and why" of notation by having them compose their own pieces.

A Variation for Sight-Singing Easy Patterns

1. Put a familiar tune on the board; sight-sing after students guess silently what the tune is.

2. Then simply change the key signature; leave the notes where they are.

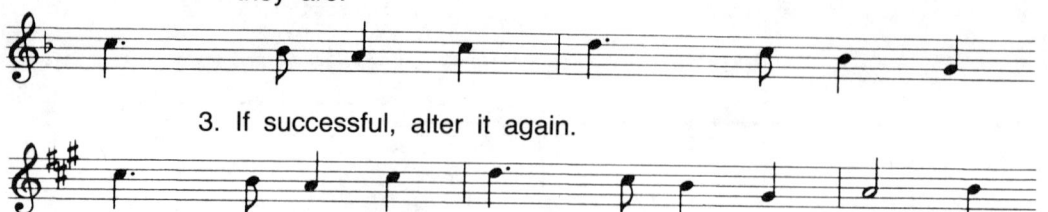

3. If successful, alter it again.

This is a useful device especially suited to the choir. You will find many students will sing it the same each time. The procedure permits a minimum amount of work at the board, and forces the singers to think of intervallic relationships within a key. Choirs generally find this enjoyable.

COMPOSITION

Ideas about what defines composition vary considerably. Usually we think of the musician engrossed in placing notes and rests on staff paper. But one can also compose by altering echo phrases, or improvising an ostinato, or inventing a simple vocal descant to a familiar song. These different interpretations of the term *composition* are fitting for the general music class. Even if you may not feel comfortable dealing with student composition, do encourage such work. While the quality of student effort may not be of a prize-winning level, composition is one more avenue toward music appreciation and interest. Let us consider some guidelines for introducing your students to the idea of composing.

Suppose that, except for one or two students who study music privately, your classes are populated with students who have never used staff paper for any reason. They have had absolutely no experience in composing music. Let us assume that you wish to introduce this activity into your class work—not as a one-shot unit but as a continuing part of your overall program. Here are some general suggestions that should help you launch this activity:

1. Insist that each composition work be *performed* by the student (if possible), or at least by someone. Do not let composition remain on paper only.
2. Limit strictly the scope of your demands. Let composition result from interest generated by the regular classroom activities.

To start with, simple echo patterns developed from rote will do. Once the class is accustomed to this, usually through purely rhythmic work, ask students to alter the echo response they provide to your lead-off. Ask for something that concludes your beginning:

(Teacher) (Student)

At first, the students' contribution should be kept to a minimum. If you choose to do melodic work, have a student complete a phrase like this:

[◄—————— teacher ——————►] [◄-student-►]

If you find it takes a while for them to listen and respond this way, do not despair. You may be the first music teacher to assign such a task. Obviously, students who cannot complete this after a few attempts will not be able to hand in homework of original, sixteen-measure melodies. If you do meet with success, gradually increase the extent of student contribution. Aim to supply, say, three measures of a tune, and ask the class for possible "answers" or concluding measures. As you keep track of the progress of each class, your demands should increase gradually and in an orderly way.

Another approach to composition is to use an "outside source" for melodic work. Most frequently used are telephone numbers. First, students are asked to write out their phone numbers. Then these numbers are translated into scale steps on the board (or on paper). So far, this activity is purely mechanical, with no musical or aesthetic element involved. Teachers sometimes quit the exercise at this point, thereby missing the essential step.

You should examine with the class several of the tone patterns, using musical criteria: balance, form, contour, range, and so on. Which phone numbers seem most complete by themselves? Which seem difficult to play or sing? What effect does applying differing rhythms have upon the patterns? Explore as many musical aspects as possible. Encourage every student to be able to play or sing his or her own number. Use one of the patterns as the first two measures of a four-measure phrase. How would the student musically complete his or her number? Do any two patterns seem to go with each other? Why? Telephone numbers are personal possessions. Like names and addresses, students' numbers are unique. This activity, by encouraging individual pride, can lead to more extensive musical involvement.

A Dictionary of Musical Themes is a worthwhile resource for pursuing classroom composition.[7] Hundreds of symphonic and vocal themes are catalogued and coded (using letter names) within the two volumes. All themes have been transposed to C and written out in letter names. You have only to rewrite any theme you wish in C and then check it against the index in

---

7. Howard Barlow and Sam Morgenstern, *A Dictionary of Musical Themes* (New York: Crown, 1957).

these books. Thus, "Twinkle, Twinkle" is CCGGAAG, and the slow section of Haydn's *Surprise Symphony* is CCEEGGE.

To start with, you may wish to pick out a few phone number patterns and compare the treatment given by students to that by serious composers using the same pattern. Tranpose any selected sequence to C and consult this encyclopedia. If you discover that Meg Brown's phone number exactly outlines the opening theme of the second movement of Brahms's *Symphony No. 2*, you have an obvious link to a listening lesson.

Other approaches might include using Social Security numbers, birth dates (for example, 4/12/19__) or even names. Schemes vary, but one could use a scheme as this: $A = 1, B = 2, C = 3, D = 4, E = 5, F = 6, G = 7, H = 1, I = 2, \ldots, Z = 5$. Then apply this code to translate names into melodies. This approach is very similar to that used frequently by serious composers (for example, "Fantasy and Fugue on B–A–C–H" by Liszt, or the "Prelude and Fugue on A–L–A–I–N" by Duruflé). In every instance, the purpose is to downplay the "gimmick" and emphasize the musical method and results. If Frank Jones discovers that Brahms's treatment of his phone number is pretty good (although he may not admit it,) your approach will have served its purpose.

If your class is receptive, you might consider having the students undertake the task of resetting a well-known TV commercial or jingle. Today's young people spend an immense amount of time watching TV, and they usually know every theme song and music track. Can the class, by group or singly, devise another Pepsi-Cola theme? Or another musical logo for a news program? Can students identify (without hearing it) TV show theme songs written on the board? How about setting some original words to music?

As you can see, there are limitless ways to incorporate composition in the general music class. Some have suggested tape recording the tone made by push-button telephones and using these sounds as raw material. Your own imagination and the general atmosphere of the class should yield numerous ideas. Remember, phone numbers or letters of names are merely springboards. It is not enough that Bill Smith realizes his name sounds like:

Does Bill grasp the musical contour of his name? Is it a pleasing tune? What would make it better? Why? Composition can be an important activity in the development of a better appreciation of music.

MOVEMENT

If you think having eighth graders compose is a challenge, wait until you say, "Everyone up. We're going to dance!" Movement to music—not as a social affair, but as a class activity—is thought to be one of the most difficult experiences to introduce and bring off. Although young people can "go wild" on the dance floor to the latest popular beat, they can be absolutely unyielding about twitching one muscle in class. After-hours rock sessions are clearly status-enhancing, socially approved activities; marching around in music class is quite another matter. Nowhere will you see peer pressure more evident than when you ask for volunteers to come to the front of the class and demonstrate a dance step. Mocking laughter often follows even the boldest soul who holds up a hand.

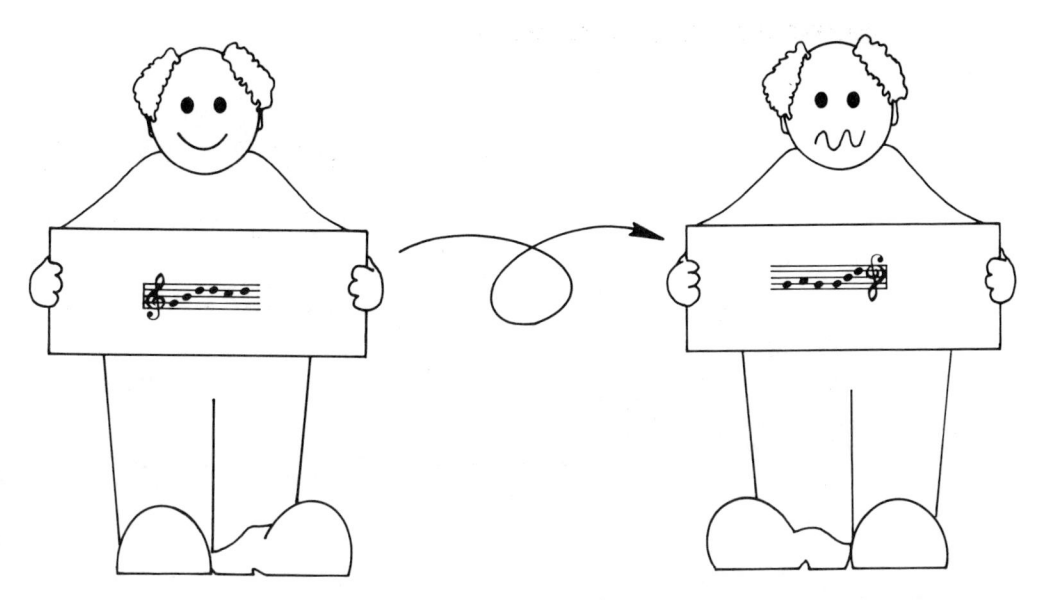

The major problem is that movement, more than any other classroom activity, is seen by students as an open invitation to look clumsy and awkward in front of friends. Of course, there are always a few students who display their seemingly absolute control over beat and body. But for most students, movement to music in class is thoroughly embarrassing. Is it any wonder, then, that their reception to your suggestions is probably going to be lukewarm at best? Badgering students or calling attention to their attitude of avoidance only makes the situation more difficult. Yet movement is enjoyable and extremely helpful in musical activities. How do you avoid this expected reluctance to participate?

The most positive stance to take is one of confidence and understanding. Throw off your own qualms about participating—be willing to get involved! Sometimes, the classroom atmosphere will be helped if you can handle in a goodnatured way the giggles and sneers about *your* ability to move. This may offset the fears of students who are reluctant to get involved. You should not expect 100% participation. Let the enjoyment shown by those who do come forward attract the more timid students.

Movement need not be viewed only as organized dances. At first, arm movement may be all you can get from a group. Let students trace a

FIGURE 5.5 *Name-the-TV-Show Game*

This requires a knowledge of the viewing habits of your particular school population. As with most of these devices, you attempt to use familiar material in order to make a point. Let them try to guess the show first; point out characteristic features, get the beat started, have them tap it out, then sing it.

melodic contour in the air with one arm. Have them sway left and right in their seats to a metric pulse. As with all activities, plan to work gradually and in a sequence toward greater involvement. Be a student yourself; many cities provide folk dance lessons through the YMCA or similar organizations. Be the first to admit that you do not know everything. Middle school students probably will be far more up-to-date than you. Learn from them. Also, consult with your colleagues in Physical Education. Often these teachers are well versed in movement, and they might agree to either visit your class or at least reinforce your efforts in their gym classes.

Sometimes, the best route is to avoid the contemporary dance scene altogether and introduce dances that are foreign to all. Line and square dances often have enormous appeal. The Jewish hora in circle fashion is extremely easy. *Consider dances that emphasize large-muscle movement, with fast pulse and easy steps.*

What musical good is added to music class through dancing or moving? Many feel that such activity is beside the point, or that music class

A simple idea with a larger class, where you wish to have them clap, tap, or drum certain rhythmic patterns. This routine gets some students up in front and has the others ready to perform. Once each card can be done independently, then the walking around aimlessly provides a randomness of arrangement when you say "STOP." If you wished, each card could show a melodic fragment from a song the students know. Can they sing it when the cards are all scrambled up?

becomes nothing more than a "fun" class and that no real musical gain can be noted. Movement may not have a direct observable effect on a student's ability to sight-read or analyze form or listen to records. However, it seems clear that writers are turning their attention more and more to the value of the sheer act of "doing":

> Mental activity . . . has its own powerful delights; but when the desire for physical activity remains unfulfilled, the basis for mental activity is considerably narrowed. Thus, the curriculum which strongly limits one aspect of human activity also limits the conditions for successful activities of other kinds.[8]

The point, in sum, is this: Do not exclude movement from general music. Even though your efforts may seem clumsy to you, persevere. Students

---

8. Beatrice Sarlos, "Learning as a Delight: The Aesthetics of Curriculum," in *Philosophers Speak of Aesthetic Experience in Education*, ed. Robert L. Leight (Danville, Ill.: The Interstate Printers & Publishers, 1975), p. 76.

unquestionably need the opportunity and experience of muscular movement to music.

Let us consider some additional practical reasons for including movement in the general music program:

1. Movement is generally accompanied by music.
2. Whether movement is gross or subtle, it provides an observable indication of the student's "feel" for pulse, tempo, and quality.
3. Success (in the student's judgment) may serve as yet another motivation to become involved in other music activities.
4. Large-muscle (whole arms, torso) movement to music is unbeatable as an introduction (or additional activity) to the art of conducting.
5. Success in movement to one rhythmic or dance pattern may foster a good attitude toward studying another movement scheme.

LISTENING

Listening has long been a part of every general music class. Along with playing, moving, creating and discussing, well-attuned ears are an important emphasis in general music instruction. The trend in recent years has been to arrange class time so that listening skills receive the greatest attention and development. Many reasons could be given for this shift in time budgeting, including the following reasons:

1. Listening is a central skill for composer, performer, and spectator alike.
2. Most people will be listeners (not performers) after graduation.
3. One can listen to and appreciate far more than he or she can perform.

There is considerable support for the idea that developing listening skills is the most logical and fitting purpose of music education. Most general music students are not in orchestras, bands, choruses or barbershop quartets. Ultimately, others will perform for them.

However, many teachers who concentrate on listening in general music may find the students' reactions and attitudes discouraging. Accustomed to listening to pop and rock radio stations, on which music selections last only a few minutes, students have acquired extremely short listening attention spans. With some notable exceptions—for example, some of the work by the Beatles, Dylan, Baez—pop music seems superficial and presents very few musical surprises, in the judgment of classically trained music educators. Too many young teachers from music conservatories look at pop music with the same analytical focus they use in examining the work of Josquin, Bach, and Stravinsky. They may react with exasperation when they realize that for three and a half minutes, the pop song uses only three chords. "Where are the subtle changes? Where does one hear the initial theme in inversion?" They expect the same sort of compositional depth in songs of Elvis Presley that they expect in Hindemith.

This is not intended as a case against pop music. In fact, it is very important for teachers to recognize the great impact of pop music upon young people, especially those in the middle school grades. The point is that your students are used to musical works of relatively short duration. These works exhibit few surprises, and they aim for immediate impact rather than for clever composition. Some pop music, however, does feature simple devices and structures. For example, teachers seeking textual AAB form can find it readily in American blues. Those looking for an abrupt modulation can find it in the Beach Boys' "Good Vibrations." Melodic phrasing can be found in Sinatra's ballads. Teachers need to be aware of what pop music has to offer, and they should present to classes only those works that clearly display basic concepts.

Use any music if it helps to clarify a point or exhibits a form/style/instrumentation/vocal quality that will aid your lesson.

Of course, always turn to worthwhile musical examples that have stood the test of time. Use the best works you can find (and this will probably mean extra listening homework for you). Get in the habit of listening to local classical FM stations. This practice will both expand your own repertoire and also provide you with opportunities to judge unfamiliar works for their classroom potential. More and more, students are denied virtually their only chance to hear fine music because teachers fail to provide frequent and varied listening experiences.

Listening Guidelines

Each week there should be time devoted to the practice of enhanced listening. No matter what the piece or movement might be, the following suggestions should assist you in making this time well-spent:

1. *duration of the work*—This refers to the actual length of the selections you wish to use. Students are used to pop pieces which average three to four minutes playing time; therefore, keep listening lessons brief and directed. Start with short works no longer than five minutes. If your students' elementary schools had programs that included practice in listening, you may be able to extend the general duration suggested. However, note that brief selections can be repeated easily within one day's lesson, whereas symphonic movements of twenty minutes cannot.

2. *source of the work*—Do not limit yourself to standard symphonic movements. Programs of major orchestras are changing, and there is a trend toward using examples from a wide range of cultures and countries. Naturally, it would be best if the listening lesson could stem directly from the work being done in class; perhaps a song could be the inspiration. At any rate, your job is to develop in students a capacity to listen to and notice musical events in the broad repertoire of world music. Music from Bali, African rhythms, European folk songs, electronic experimentation, and so forth should augment your core of listening examples.

3. *approach to the work*—Of central importance is your own familiarity with the pieces. As you listen, jot down the most apparent aspects of the piece: its melody, form, rhythm. Note, too, the less obvious aspects: a hidden canon or a disguised nursery tune. Establish a ranking of musical events. Let this act as the structure around which you organize your lesson. By choosing pieces that are short, you can plan for at least two complete playings of the piece and probably several opportunities to hear other portions of the work. Build from the whole to the parts and then back to the whole again.

To implement this, consider using the following approach. It is best to use a full score. You will learn the piece better yourself and you will be able to provide an accurate analysis for the pupils. Play your selection, listen, and follow the score. Your focus will be on tone color and, perhaps, tempo. Whenever something of musical importance occurs—a change, a deletion, an addition—lightly jot a number under that measure in the score. Limit your numbers to the obvious at first. Be sure to keep the numbers spread out if possible, especially in fast-tempo works.

On paper, list the numbers and next to each indicate in simple terms what is happening. Make copies of the list and pass them out to the class. With score in hand, play the disc and call out the numbers. Students will read what you have written, and you avoid having to shout over the sounds to tell them what is going on. Your "call chart" might look like this:

Overture Breve

Call No.	Measure No.	Events
1	1	full orchestra; forte; fast
2	4	strings only; quiet; slow
3	6	new idea in oboe; flute echoes
4	9	original theme in cello
5	11	coda; cello and oboe themes

When you are finished and want to know if the students heard what you described in this call chart, make up a "test chart." It would look something like this:

1	full orchestra forte slow		brass only piano fast
2	bassoons only fast		strings only slow
3	same theme solo in flute	in oboe	new theme in violin
4	brass has the theme		theme in cello
5	new theme one theme only		themes heard before several themes at once

The students circle or underline their choices as you call the number. This approach helps you determine the degree to which they are hearing what they should. Have them check their answers by replaying the disc and following the chart again. If you wish, have them pass in their graded tests. This will enable you to keep a record of the progress of each student.

Such a procedure provides the repetition so necessary and helps to improve the limiting "hearing" of most students. Have them (*a*) listen to the whole piece, (*b*) pick it apart, (*c*) point out parts, (*d*) listen to the parts, (*e*) discuss them, and then (*f*) listen to the entire selection again. The more one knows about something, the better he or she will be able to judge and appreciate it. With this type of lesson, students can base their comments on experience and insight rather than sheer emotion or surface impact.

Your responsibility is to provide the young listeners with a road map to follow, by asking good questions and by pointing out what there is to attend to. Establish some questions to ask *before* the first playing, such as "What instruments do you hear? Does this move in 2 or 3?" Keep the first questions simple and don't ask too many, but do ask them. Always give students something specific to listen *for* every time they listen—not just the overall effect.

One of the major shortcomings in listening lessons has been lack of opportunity to determine whether the students actually have heard what teachers wanted them to hear. Did they hear the second part? Did they hear the trumpet? How will you ever know? Many students will say or do whatever they think is expected by the teacher. Ask specifics: "Was the solo by a flute or an oboe? Was this in ABA or rondo form?" Avoid the whole issue of "Do you like this or not?"—your job is not to turn music into a popularity contest.

Using charts such as those shown previously is attention-getting and beneficial in the classroom. Remember, this is only a suggested paper-and-pencil tool to determine the listening skills of the class. Variations on this approach are limitless. You might choose to prepare overhead transparencies. Let the students devise their own listening charts, or have them graph a piece using dots, lines, colors, diagrams or geometric shapes.

Your concern is to sharpen an ability, not to dictate your own preferences to the class. Be enthusiastic and down-to-earth; show students that there are aspects of the chosen work that appeal to everybody.

The guidelines for a successful listening lesson are simple and few:

1. Keep the piece fairly short so that you can repeat it during the lesson.
2. Search around for variety in your selections, always in the market for the unusual and captivating.
3. Maintain your own mental storehouse of examples by putting on the earphones regularly.
4. Test students on what you want them to hear.
5. Provide for quick musical success.

Questions & Activities

1. Students bring their rock records to class on Friday. "Mrs. Romero always let us play our records." You are unfamiliar with just about all of the titles, yet the students are clamoring to hear them. What do you do?
2. One of the boys in class volunteers to play a piece, one he has worked on for his private lessons. However, he plays very poorly, with mistakes so obvious that the class snickers. How would you handle this situation?
3. Visit a local middle school and ask permission to test the voices of some of the students. Check your results with the music teacher.
4. Set your own name or telephone number to music and see what you can do with it. Share your efforts with the class.
5. Develop your own scheme of notation. Try it out with the class. If successful, get permission to introduce it to a neighborhood middle school class.

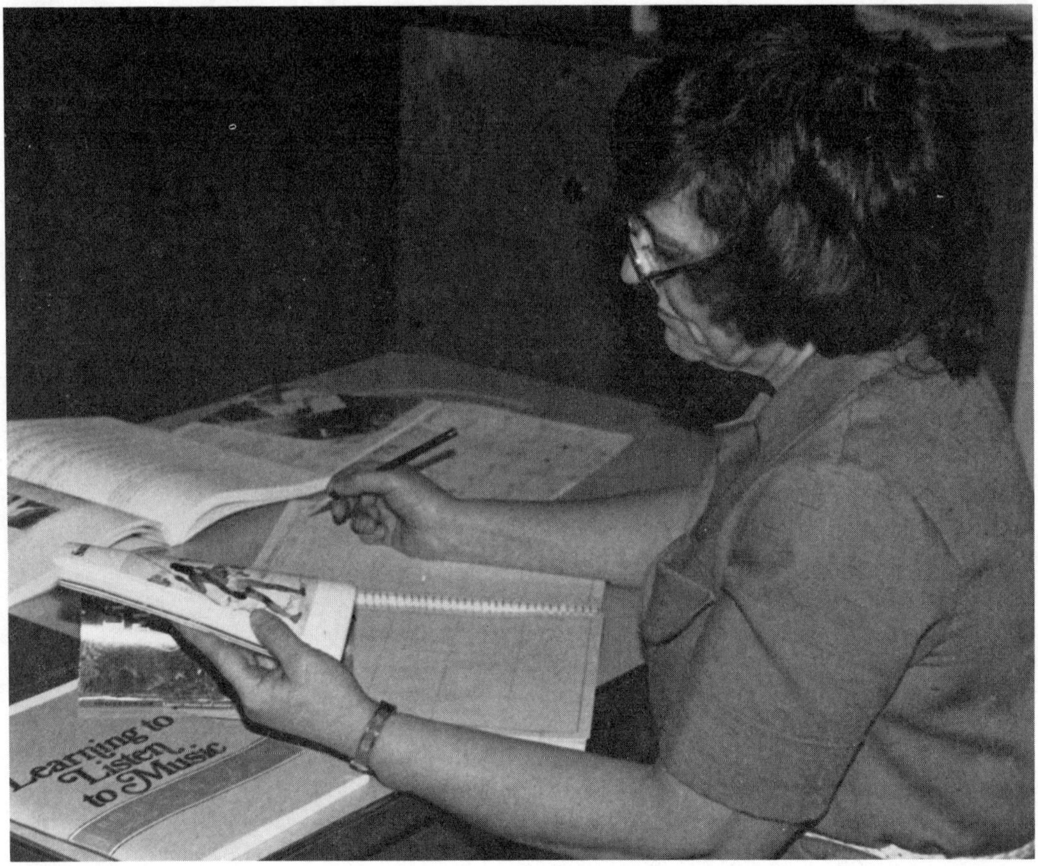
Learning to
Listen
to Music

That's the reason they're called lessons, because they lessen from day to day.

Lewis Carroll

Lesson Planning 6

Music education seeks qualified people who wish to go beyond the concert hall to the classroom. Being an exceptionally good trumpeter or soprano does not, however, insure that one will also be an effective music teacher. Part of your preparation for teaching is training in planning lessons that are purposeful, active, involving, and goal-directed. In fact, planning a single class is as demanding as any task given a musician-teacher. The ability to plan with purpose and focus is often singled out as the factor which best describes the truly effective teacher. It is fitting, therefore, that we turn now to some approaches to planning a general music class.

STRUCTURING THE LESSON PLAN

The Sonata-Allegro Method

The most pressing problem facing the new teacher is simply what to do. Suddenly, you face thirty or more students on opening day. You recognize that the musical fate of many of these students is in your hands; you seek answers to immediate problems. Your own preparation is the single most powerful tool at your disposal. Even experienced teachers need to think through what they are going to do and what they are after. To be sure, all teachers have "blue" days when the clock runs backwards, all the top students are discipline problems, and you have two fire drills that were not announced. But these days can be kept to a minimum by a simple idea, a notion which stems from the art itself: *Plan the lesson just as you would compose something in sonata-allegro form.*

Let us examine what this idea means. How does one treat the sonata form? What features does it have? Four major portions can be easily translated into methodology: (*a*) introduction, (*b*) thematic statement, (*c*) development, and (*d*) recapitulation.

The *introduction* is a brief segment designed either to catch our attention or to give us a preview of the mood and direction of the work. The introduction is brief but purposeful: It sets the climate (important both in music and in classroom management). Then comes the *statement* section, in which two or more ideas are presented. These ideas are given in their original musical form and are connected by some sort of a bridge section. They may or may not be repeated. Then the "real work" gets under way: The composer shows his or her skill in the *development* of musical ideas—changing them, combining them, abbreviating them, and so on. The path may stray, but in the *recapitulation* we hear those original tunes once again, just as they were at the start. This section makes sense, both musically and psychologically, for it mirrors the whole–part–whole approach. The return of the original material confirms the musical premise stated at the start; our senses are gratified by the return, and we say "Ah, there it is again." Finality thus is achieved. What has this to do with our music class? Let us examine now how these four portions can be related to classroom management.

Introduction

The introduction may be catchy or it may set the mood for what follows. Whichever function it serves, it should be related to that which follows. Jumping out the window would be catchy, but not (perhaps) directly related to the day's lesson; draping the room in black and wearing a long face would help establish a dismal mood in class, but it would be rather pointless if it has no musical application. Your introduction stems directly from the lesson for the day. To be catchy, it may be amusing, thought-provoking, a complete change of pace, or something else. Every lesson establishes its own boundaries and possibilities; your own imagination is essential here.

Devise some means of attracting the class at the start. Compel the class to pay attention because of what you do or say. Compress your introduction so that it does not take up an hour's time, but merely sets the stage. Some examples will clarify this: The moment the class is quiet, play a series of tone clusters on the piano. You turn and ask, "Is that music?" Or begin the class by reading some account from the newspaper, and then relate it to a song they are about to sing. Have the lights dimmed prior to their entrance and begin to discuss the use of light and shadow (for example) in painting. Enact, with the help of some students, the form of a fugue as you and these assistants mime certain movements. Read the text of a song about to be sung as if it were a poem, and discuss its merits and values as poetry. The point is that a certain amount of *drama* in the classroom can be invaluable, and your skill in bringing off such an approach can have considerable worth. As a rule, "inventing" your introduction comes last in the planning scheme. Establish your objectives and content first; then devise an introduction appropriate to the focus of the lesson.

Statement of Themes

Once you have the attention of the class, turn immediately to the business at hand. By *themes* is meant the focus or conceptual content of the day's work. The sonata may offer the listener a fast, light theme and a slower, heavier one; similarly, the teacher provides variety in every class by submitting for study several diverse topics or musical concepts. They should lend themselves to different kinds of activities. Perhaps one idea will require discussion while another will demand physical activity. Both are necessary features in the middle school class. Never let it be *all* one thing. Too much talk (in particular) or singing or listening can spoil the class.

Explore two or three basic concepts in each class. The concepts frequently will be simple—for example, differences in musical texture, or the effect of high and low on a melody. New teachers often misunderstand the term *concept* and feel they must state some lofty, all-encompassing goal in their plans. Quite the opposite is true. Limit yourself as much as possible; the more tightly you plan, the more freedom you will have to pursue class work. Further, the use of several different themes in your class takes into account the very short attention span of most students in these grades.

Your foremost goal is to enhance appreciation of and sensitivity to sound and silence. There can be no set timetable for this. Every day you explore something musical, pressing onward without the idea that the "material must be covered." For example, let us suppose you establish two objectives for the class:

1. to define, discuss, and play the perfect fourth (P4) and to be able to hear it in a short melodic passage
2. to continue work on good vocal production through use of some familiar songs

Your first objective involves work on the blackboard, the piano, the tone bells, and so on. You will show the students how the P4 is formed, how it sounds; you will have them sing it from various starting tones. Their work will be reinforced as they listen to, perhaps, both a melody by you that uses the fourth and a recording of chant or rock ballads incorporating the same interval. *All activities revolve around the same concept.* The results will probably be less than perfect at first. That is all right, for you will return some other day to review the fourth and refresh the memories of the group. Before you leave interval work for the period, try to establish how much the students have gained so far—a quick verbal restatement, a short series of intervals played (seconds, fourths, sevenths, and so on) in which they pick out the fourths. Then you move on to the second objective—singing. Your focus now is on developing an assured, unembarrassed approach to singing. Remember, the general music class is not the choir. Seek to get *most* of the students to feel free enough to take part in vocal music. Consider yourself lucky to get this much.

Development of Themes

The development section of your lesson, involving the activities that you use to make your point, merges with the statement section. Every concept that you investigate will suggest numerous approaches. Sometimes the *deductive* approach will be best—that is, stating the general idea first, then exploring the details. Other times, the *inductive* method will fit—presenting the details or specifics first, and then drawing them together at the close by pointing out the common thread that unites all the details. Other times, you will find that the so-called *discovery* approach is best. The problem with this latter method is that it is often approached with some prior assumption about what the class should "discover." To be more rewarding, discovery learning should lead off into tangents that may or may not have relevance to the general topic.[1] To follow this path, you should be creative enough to feel comfortable pursuing ideas that seem to come "out of left field." Whatever method you use, keep in mind at all times where it is you want to go.

As you develop the themes, keep talk to an absolute minimum. Definitions, of course, require language that is clear, descriptive, and free from personal interpretations and biases. However, most of the time in class should be taken up in experimenting with sound and silence. Develop the ability to relate the subject at hand to everyday life. Thus, as Bernstein has done, you could use a baseball diamond to illustrate the history and development of intervals and scales.[2] This analogy has a better chance of conveying your point than some theoretical, nonspecific lecture. There will be

---

1. See Charles Fowler, "Discovery Method, Its Relevance for Music Education," *Journal of Research in Music Education* 14, no. 2 (Summer 1966): 126–34.
2. Leonard Bernstein, *The Joy of Music* (New York: Simon & Schuster, 1959), p. 191.

many times when classes come alive discussing musical matters and recognizing that music presents quite an intellectual challenge. Nontheless, as a rule, keep talking short and to the point.

Recapitulation

Once the composer has exhausted his or her work with sonata themes and has gone far afield displaying them in various ways, the composer brings them back at the close of the piece. So, too, you should plan your time so that every class includes some opportunity to review what was done. This need not be long and involved; it seeks simply to promote closure by integrating earlier work. It puts the little pieces back together again.

The review, or recapitulation, will feature the same behaviors called upon during the class. For example, if recognition by ear of the plagal cadence has been one of your themes, and the class work has involved records, the piano, tone bars, and the autoharp, your review will use these same instruments. You could ask a student to come up and play a plagal cadence on the keyboard if the student has had a chance to practice it during the class.

Accomplishment of fairly easy, short-term objectives is very much a part of teaching music. Such small successes, day after day, will help to create a confident, positive atmosphere. Understand, too, that every class need not spend its last four minutes talking about what has transpired. No timetable should be followed strictly; however, the recapitulation section of your class should be near the end of class.

IMPLEMENTING THE LESSON PLAN

When we think of planning, we usually think of the classroom teacher in the elementary school—the teacher who must handle the math, English, social studies and history all by herself or himself. For this kind of teacher, planning is absolutely necessary. Musicians, however, view planning differently because they were trained as performers, and their schooling in the art was perhaps restricted to technique and repertoire. As students, we may have thought about our music teachers not as planners but rather as people who guided our practice and interpretations. Private lessons in applied music are private matters and do not exhibit those characteristics of planning we associate with the classroom. Therefore, many of us would do well to consider the classroom teacher to see what we can learn from him or her.

Instead of facing eager private students, we get students who show differing attitudes toward music. To plan, we must know (a) why we are in front of the class in the first place and (b) what we wish to teach. In dealing with general music, instrumental ensemble, or appreciation class, music teachers must understand some basics of planning and must learn to view plans as useful tools toward an end.

Good lessons have specific *objectives*. The necessary *materials* are well chosen and handy. The lesson *content* consistently points toward and clarifies the objective. The day's conclusions are stated and *reviewed*. From these points we can construct a simple planning framework enabling us to plug in ideas.

Objectives

Good lesson plans spell out the objectives clearly and simply. Anyone can write an objective; the challenge is to word it so that it can be pursued realistically. Objectives should be stated simply and be consistent with the overriding philosophy. Thus, "to study the musical textures available to a composer, and to be able to aurally differentiate them" are objectives that can be implemented and measured. Let us proceed in this vein further: "to appreciate music" or "to hear tone color" (too vague); "to compare pop music with the classics" (compare in what way?); "to understand form in music" (too broad, and impossible to grasp what "understand" means to the planner). If your stated objective seems picky or narrow, that's fine—it should be. Most classes need repetition and constant review, and so expansive objectives are thoroughly impractical. In sum, objectives are short, clear statements about which you gear the hour's time.

Materials

Every lesson (that is, the whole class time) requires some materials, be they books or records or blackboard. Plans should state clearly what you will need in order to teach the lesson. Again, these should be specific statements about which book, what page, which record, etc. Materials are usually stated at the top of the plan, next to the objectives. Remember, someday you may wish to repeat your presentation. Will you be able to do so, following your own plan? Is it specific enough? This is particularly important for records and songs—always list the title, page number, movement, disc label, and so forth in your materials. It is better to err on the side of being overly specific rather than not specific enough.

Content

The greatest amount of time in planning goes to content. This is the meat of your lesson—the questions, the timing, the activities, the analogies. Success or failure usually hinges on the quality of this section. It was suggested earlier that you should devise a lead-off or introductory statement that will interest, attract, or perplex the class. *Unpredictability* is one of your most powerful tools.

The content section is not a script, but rather a body of carefully thought-out questions or problems that you will pose to the class. Phrase your questions with a vocabulary suitable for the group; as a rule, be simple and straightforward. List the major questions and the activities that apply. By *activities* is meant the whole gamut of physical and verbal "doing" that is so essential in middle school. Many lessons get bogged down not because of examples or songs but because the students have nothing to do but listen to and look at you. "Doing" means responding to and handling musical materials—hitting a tone bar, strumming an autoharp, or stating an opinion of how well or how poorly the music and text went together. "Doing" means involving the students in something constructive, and it is a feature of every effective lesson.

Too many college people approach the music class as an opportunity to lecture to youngsters; then they find that the responsiveness they had anticipated is nil. The lecture method usually is inapplicable at this level. Some classes are quite bright, of course, but these young students still need verbal and physical involvement. Failure to provide this involvement can lead to discipline problems.

Which activities work? What sort of involvement is worthwhile? All classes differ in certain respects, but a few activities seem to be relevant generally:

1. singing with a purpose, aware of good and poor sound
2. moving some part(s) of the body
3. discussing visual aids
4. clapping and speaking rhythmic phrases
5. playing and improvising on whatever instruments are available

Singing, perhaps the most natural activity in class, must be viewed as an activity in which great diversity in performance is acceptable. Many boys will suffer through the voice change and will be inhibited about singing, especially alone. Seek a healthy, responsive output. Achieve this, *then* turn attention to proper intonation.

Moving is highly recommended and should be encouraged whenever possible. Again, inhibition is a problem. Perhaps rocking in the seat or raising and lowering the arm within a 4/4 meter is all you can get. Get the rhythmic response into the large muscles as often as possible. Involve the class in activities that appeal as much to the body as to the mind.

Students are visually oriented because of their TV-viewing habits. Sometimes you can devise large visual aids for discussion (see Figure 5.4 in Chapter 5). These aids make use of the blackboard unnecessary and save a great deal of time. Texture, for example, is an element easily given over to visual graphs and pictures. To discuss verbally the difference between homophonic and polyphonic textures may result in responses less satisfactory than if you had approached the textures with 〰〰 and 〰 .

Clapping and/or speaking patterns is yet another way to get students to participate. You could easily start a rhythmic round or rhythmic echo sequence, just as elementary teachers do.

Playing anything, whether a tone bar or a violin, appeals to one's sense of touch. Musical sound-producers are limited only by your own imagination. Hub caps and rubber bands and old brake drums have been used successfully. No budget and no instruments? Let the students bring in junk, and from that construct your own "orchestra." Let the Masters come in *after* your students have tried music making on their own, without preconceived notions and limitations. Surely, common sense dictates that whenever possible, students should explore good instruments (for example, wooden recorders, not plastic) and properly tuned keyboards. The point is that lack of well-crafted, in-tune instruments should not impede the general music class.

Review

Every class ought to have a few moments for retrospect. When the clock shows about five minutes left, stop the activity, allow for the instruments to be put away, and spend a little time talking about what had been discussed and learned. Review is needed during the class, at the end of class, and sometimes at the start of the next class.

"What does this word [point to word on board] mean? Which of the two I'm about to play at the piano fills the bill? What did we decide *homophonic* meant? Is this homophonic? Christina, come here and play those three bars [c-e-g]—is that a triad or not? If I sing ♩ ♩ ♩ ♩ ♩ would you say that is legato or staccato? Here's a rock group doing a piece that you all know. Is the melody constant, or does it come in and out? Are you sure of that? Let's check to make sure. Is this tone higher or lower than this one? Bruce, that was a very good answer. If you wanted to write a piece that was brisk and dancelike, which instruments would you choose? What tempo would you select?" The quality of the questions you ask is important not only for review but throughout the entire lesson.

Review should be more than mere repetition of terms and definitions done in class. It involves repetition, of course, but this can be managed in various ways. Aside from purely oral feedback from students, simple quizzes can be used to measure whether or not your points were made. (If you do not know the degree to which the objective was realized, tomorrow's lesson might be no more than a variation of today's.) Testing may be based on (*a*) students' recognition of aspects of records or songs you have played or (*b*) purely verbal descriptions and definitions.

Don't jump the moment one student gives a correct answer. Ask, "Are you certain?" or stall your reply and call on a few others. If a student is almost to the answer, do not say "Well, almost," and move on—stay with him or her a bit and make him do better, be more specific. Show that you are aware of students' remarks and that you evaluate the accuracy of their answers. If a student comes around, give positive reinforcement; praise even the most feeble effort if it is well meant, resourceful, and imaginative.

Demonstrate that little things from students mean a lot. Call on students by name. As much as possible, show a personal interest in individuals. For example, use the board to list terms or show diagrams. As you finish, return to them and point at them as you ask, "What does this mean, Ramon?" or "Venetia, do you recall what this drawing had to do with the Bach piece?"

Find a new work that contains the same qualities discussed in class. As a review, play it and see if the class can spot that same device in the new work. If they can, you have taught well enough for that listening skill to transfer to new works, and this is very good. Have the class repeat orally new terms, especially foreign-language words. Spell them slowly on the board. Give clear examples of how they sound or how they apply to music. Even as the lesson unfolds, take a moment to ask, "What did we say this meant, again?" It may seem tedious and redundant to you. Nonetheless, review and repetition are essential aspects of teaching.

Questions & Activities

1. This chapter suggested that the sonata-allegro form may offer a logical scheme for developing a lesson plan. Investigate other approaches and report to class.

2. "If you save all your lessons this year, you can simply repeat them next year." Discuss the benefits and drawbacks of this idea.

3. Mursell often spoke of "incidental" learning as being important in music class. What is "incidental" learning, and how would one go about providing it?

4. *TV Guide* indicates that next Sunday, Leonard Goodfellow will conduct a Young Persons' Concert. The topic will be "Modern Music." Your musical heart leaps in rapture. You decide to assign your classes to watch. Then, you discover that opposite the concert is the Pro-Bowl game. Do you:

    a. assign everyone to watch the concert as an obligatory activity?
    b. make it merely a suggestion?
    c. assign certain volunteers to watch and report?
    d. none of these?

    Consider other options, and how you would plan for Monday's class.

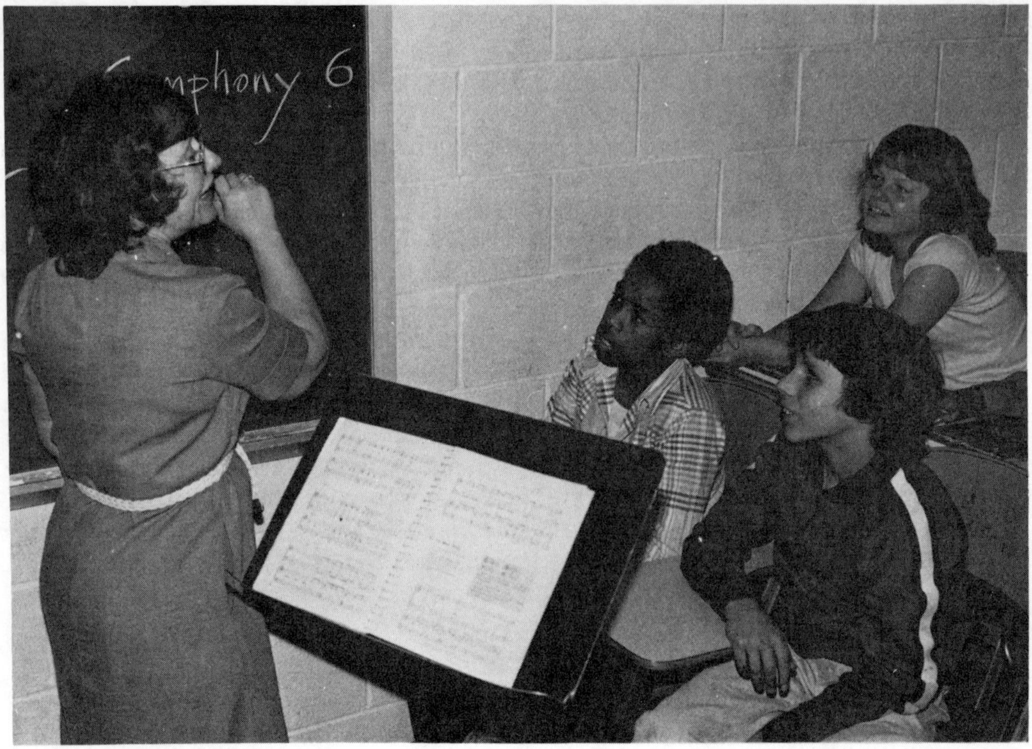
mphony 6

Sample Lesson Plans

7

This chapter contains lesson plans developed in the junior high general music class. The lessons are intended to provide the detail and organization often needed by undergraduate music education majors. The length of these lessons is to be seen not as a model, but as representing a series of quasi-scripts which might be used just as they read.

Ideally, a good lesson plan is short, direct, and "custom made." Abbreviations and marginal notes frequently appear on plans devised for the eyes of the experienced teacher. However, the novice needs as much step-by-step direction as possible. With experience, lesson planning should become easier. The purpose of these lessons is to give the novice something to study. These lessons are not intended to replace those already available in series books. Rather, they should act as a skeletal frame which can be filled in as the teacher adds additional plans. In-service music teachers can easily alter these plans to suit their unique needs. "Student plan" pages are included so that the reader can expand and develop those concepts approached in these lesson plans.

LESSON PLAN 1   MELODY

OBJECTIVES
to define *melody*; to explore melodic contour and phrases

MATERIALS
xylophone; large chart with "Dona Nobis Pacem"

Introduction

"How are you today?" Say it, then sing it immediately.

(musical notation: "How are you to-day?")

"How were these statements the same, and different?" Get answers. "Let's go one step further. How are *these* the same, and different?"

(musical notation: "I am fine thank you.")

(musical notation: "I am fine thank you.")

(Both use same text; both were sung; first version is all one tone, while second is melodic.) Lead discussion to a definition of **melody.**

Content

"*Melody* [put word on board] is a series of musical tones that go somewhere. Melodies usually rise and fall, and in a song they let the words come through with an impact different than if the words were merely said.

"Trace with your hand in the air the ups and downs of these melodies." Play three, or four tunes, at least two of which are well known—such as "Star Spangled Banner," current pop tune, "America," and the like. Check the traced contours as you play the melodies.

"The invisible outline of these melodies is called the *contour* [write word on board] of the melody. What are some words we can use to describe the contour of melodies?" Write responses on the board, e.g., jagged, smooth, flowing, jumpy, long, short, etc. Select three or four of these suggested terms and check to see how well the class can describe the following melodies:

Improvise on piano (or xylophone) some melodies that are obviously different in contour from one another. Can the class identify a jagged melody from a smooth one? Ask for three volunteers to trace with chalk at the board the melodies you play.

"Now we'll reverse the game. I'll draw a contour on the board and ask you to sing/play your own melodic interpretation." Do only about three of these, such as the following:

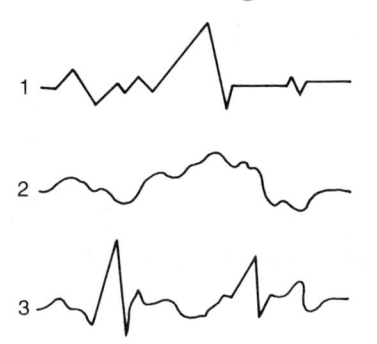

Use piano or a tuned bar instrument.

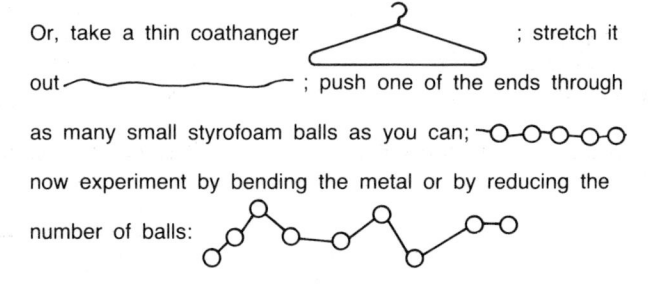

Or, take a thin coathanger   ; stretch it out   ; push one of the ends through as many small styrofoam balls as you can;   now experiment by bending the metal or by reducing the number of balls:

Use this simple visual aid to check the ability of your class to interpret this variable "contour form" through singing/xylophone/piano. Let students alter the form and then create a musical interpretation.

"Notice that no matter what actual tones are heard, the shape or contour of each melody has a special 'feel' or quality about it. Composers have to be aware of this, and arrange their melodies to capture the quality they want. The melodic contour [point to word on board] is an important musical quality—one that both classical and popular composers need to understand and that listeners should observe as they listen.

Lesson Plan 1   Melody

"Most melodies, especially those that have words (a text) with them, are created by arranging the tones of a selected scale to suit both text and composer. Instead of writing any old notes one after another, melodies are usually written to spotlight important words, to start from here, go to there (but not sound finished yet), repeat the general contour of the opening note series, and then finish with a last, conclusive idea. These parts of the overall melody are called *phrases* [write word on board]. A phrase is a musical idea, rather complete by itself. When put with other phrases that are similar, we have a complete melody—a whole musical idea.

"To show what I mean, let's return to the way I started class today. 'How are you today?' is a phrase. It seems to need some kind of answer. One I gave was, 'I am fine, thank you.' Let's musically trace how those own ideas might look."

On the board:

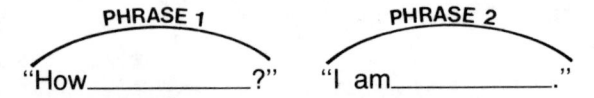

```
      PHRASE 1              PHRASE 2
   ⌢⌢⌢⌢⌢⌢⌢           ⌢⌢⌢⌢⌢⌢⌢
"How_____?"      "I am_____."
```

"The first half asks, or says something incomplete; the second answers. Let's see if you can just give me some spoken answers to what I say."

Using simple questions, see if the students can orally respond like this:

Teacher	Volunteer
"How cold is it today?"	"It's very cold."
"What color is your shirt?"	"My shirt is_____."
"The sky is blue and clear."	"The clouds seem bright and near."

"How do musical questions and answers sound? Here's a simple example:

(CWM RHONDDA)

Q ———————————————— ?   A ————————————————

"Let's sing something with regular, balanced phrases or parts to it, such as 'Barb'ra Allen' or 'The Water is Wide.'[1] Let's look at the latter.

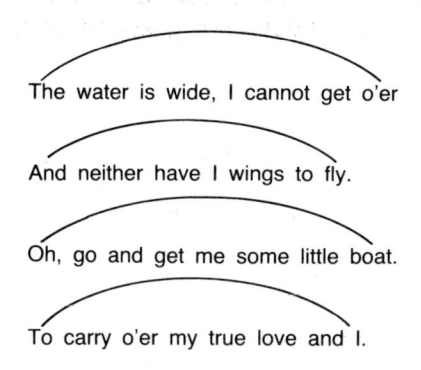

⌒
The water is wide, I cannot get o'er

⌒
And neither have I wings to fly.

⌒
Oh, go and get me some little boat.

⌒
To carry o'er my true love and I.

"How does it sound or feel if we stop after 'wings to fly'? Does it sound completed? If not, what does it need? Why does it sound as though it needs to go longer before it's done?

"You've all heard about musical scales before. One thing you should understand about scales and the tones that make them up is this: In most of the scale arrangements (melodies) we hear, some tones sound final, some really leave you hanging, and others can work both ways. Let's see how this works."

Play a major scale on B♭ below middle C. Have class sing on numbers, up and down. Now have them sing from #1 to #7 and stop. Ask for reactions (do *not* play or sing #8). Can they feel the pull of #7 wanting to finish up on #8? Do the same, singing down from #8 to #2. Does #2 want to move somewhere? Discuss this magnetism and illustrate how the answer to a "questioning" phrase seems to want to return to the stable tones of the scale.

Write on board:

• = stable
o = wants to move
∞ = works both ways

1 2 3 4 5 6 7 8 (1)

---

1. "The Water is Wide," which is in the public domain, can be found in Reimer et al., *Silver Burdett Music, Grade 7* (Morristown, N.J.: Silver Burdett, 1975), p. 63.

Lesson Plan 1   Melody

"Let's apply what we've discussed to music. We'll make those spoken sentences we did earlier into musical phrases. Using the same words, I'll sing the first phrase, start the answer phrase, and ask you to complete it. Make your ending sound finished."

Teacher . . . . (Student completes - ?)

"How cold is it to - day?"   "It's ver - - - - y cold."

"What co - lor is your shirt?"   "My shirt is col - ored blue."

"The sky is blue and clear,   the clouds seem bright and near."

"To review our work on melodies and phrases, we'll examine a well-known tune that is usually sung as a round [review term if necessary]. As you listen, note first the contour of the melody. If you wish, graph it on paper at your desk."

"Dona Nobis Pacem" (sing/play/use recording)

Have a large poster ready with this melody notated on it. "How would you describe the contour of that melody [smooth, some leaps, mostly stepwise]? Now we'll see what that melody looks like." Introduce the large poster now.

Sample Lesson Plans   93

[Musical notation: Three systems of music with lyrics "Do-na no-bis pa-cem pa-cem Do-na no-bis pa-cem" repeated across the staves, in 3/4 time with one flat key signature.]

"As I play it again, raise your hand when you think the first phrase stops, or tell which syllable it ends on. When you do and we agree on it, a volunteer will color that note in colored chalk." Have class follow chart. When done, ask how many phrases altogether there are. Do all the "question" phrases have an "answer"? Sing the melody without splitting into parts. Save the round idea for later. "Observe how the colored chalk notes finish the question phrases. They are restless tones, or 'unstable.'" Point out that (*a*) phrase #1 ends on the seventh scale step, (*b*) phrase #3 ends on the second step, and (*c*) phrase #5 ends on the fifth step (a note that works either way).

Review

"Let's review what we've done today:

1. What is a melody?
2. What do we call the shape of a melody?
3. What is a phrase? Can one simply speak a phrase? [Try it.]

Lesson Plan 1   Melody

"While not every melody is composed to fit into such a neat formula of ? and !, enough have been that we can see how composers think about arranging tones. The rise and fall of notes is important to them and to us. Upward-moving notes feel one way, and notes that move downward affect us differently. Remember *contour* and *phrase*. We'll be using these words next time when we talk about how composers stretch their melodies to make them last longer.

"To finish today, let's sing a song you all know—'I Love the Mountains.'[2] As you sing it, try to feel how each phrase of the melodic contour builds up."

---

2. This song, which is in the public domain, can be found in Lawrence Eisman, Elizabeth Jones, and Raymond J. Malone, *Making Music Your Own* (Morristown, N.J.: Silver Burdett, 1968), pp. 138–39.

LESSON PLAN 2   MELODY

OBJECTIVES

to review *contour* and *phrase*; to introduce and define *sequence* in melody

MATERIALS

Bach, Fantasy in C
"I Love The Mountains"
Pezel, Suite ("Sarabande")

Introduction

"The detective said, 'Let's see if I have this right. First, the suspect acted funny in the bar. Then, he punched someone next to him and ran out. Next, he was seen running along the sidewalk to a waiting car, punching people as he ran. Loud yelling was heard and the car took off. Someone saw him punch the driver. Is that the sequence of events, Lieutenant?'

"What do we mean by the word *sequence?*" Accept something like a pattern, or a logical chain of events linked together.

Content

"Composers use the idea of sequence in music very often. Today, we'll try to build some musical sequences ourselves and hear how others have used this technique to stretch out their compositions. To make sure you understand what a sequence in music sounds like, listen to this:

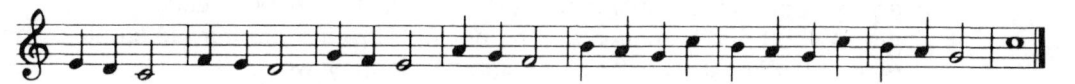

What was the pattern, or sequence, in that? Who can sing/graph it?
"On the board, it would look like this:

In numbers, it would be 3–2–1, 4–3–2, 5–4–3, 6–5–4 and so on. The small idea or 'motif' of 3–2–1 is the heart of this sequence. Using it in different ways, a composer can stretch out and add unity to this composition.

"Here's an example of the use of sequence. Listen, and be able to sing or graph the pattern that is used over and over. Try to listen to the first few notes especially."

Bach's Fantasy in C, for organ

Lesson Plan 2   Melody

[musical notation]

Get responses from class about the shape of the sequences.
"You could have a sequence in harmony or rhythm, too, but usually we think of a melodic pattern that repeats over and over. Here's another.

"I Love the Mountains"[3]

[musical notation]

"How was sequence used here?" Get responses from class. Look for them to sing it back, or graph it, or show with hand motion the flow of the sequence. Note pattern in the first four tones of each phrase. "Let's define sequence again." Lead to a working statement that it is a pattern—usually melodic—that is short and is moved up and down. "Now it's your turn to create some sequences to show you understand how they work."

Option 1

Have students either individually or by small group create short, sequential schemes using preestablished motifs, shown as either graphs or actual notation. Thus, students select one of these and work from it:

[musical notation]

Performance should be vocal/keyboard/tone bars/glock.

---
3. In Eisman, Jones, and Malone, *Making Music Your Own*, p. 138.

Option 2

Have students individually or by small group create their own sequences without suggestion from you. For either approach, suggest that the melodic *contour* be easy to hear and move around. Review *phrase;* the sequential patterns should not mechanically move higher/lower but should be grouped into phrases.

With all student performances, insist on close peer attention and solicit comments about the quality of each performance. If possible, have all groups perform in the same day. Do not postpone their chance to demonstrate. Consider taping some of the examples. A particularly good job could provide the content for an extended follow-up lesson.

"What does the use of sequence add to a melody? Let's make up some phrases that have absolutely no relationship to one another. We'll avoid any repetition and sequences and see if our phrases seem to make musical sense. To help, I'll make up a few doodles and then try to play them. When I'm done, you'll do the same thing."

On board, invent something like this:

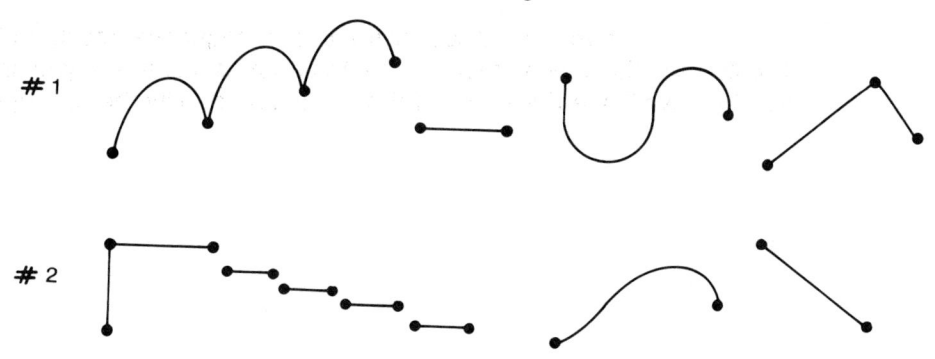

#1

#2

Now interpret vocally/instrumentally as your imagination dictates. The point is that without repetition or sequence the melody does not give us much to hang onto or to remember. It is a negative approach, one to be used infrequently. But in this case, it might be helpful. Next, students invent the same type of nonrepetitive doodles and perform them.

"Now, let's return to the first set of squiggles. How could we develop a sequence out of this?" Have any suggestion performed in class. Some might look to the repetition and movement of the first idea ᨇ as one to use. Try out all of them.

"Can sequence be found in art?" Draw some simple sequential patterns (e.g., o-o o-o-oo-o o-o o-o or ▫▯▯▫▯▯▫▯▯ ▫▯ ?). "Can we find sequence in the world around us? In the classroom? The school building?"

Discuss these possibilities. "Buildings, paintings, poems, sculpture—all the arts use sequences, because people have always felt the need for some pattern in their lives. It is easy to pick out the repetitions in paintings or billboards because we can look at and study them at our leisure. But music is different: Because it moves in *time*, not space, listeners need to have some pattern, some musical idea that returns over and over so they can remember it. It makes sense, then, that sequences are extremely important to us; the songs we sing, the pieces we play here, our dance steps all make use of sequence."

Review

"We've talked about three terms today: contour, phrase, and sequence. Who can define each one? Who can demonstrate each one? Let's conclude by hearing a short piece that uses sequence frequently, and see how it fits into the whole scheme."

Pezel's Suite ("Sarabande")[4]

"If you can discover the use of sequence, motif, and so on in Top 40 selections, bring them to me. I'll check to make sure you are correct, and then we'll see if the rest of the class can identify the concept in use."

---

4. *Learning to Listen to Music* (Morristown, N. J.: Silver Burdett, 1969), Record IV, Side 1, Band 1.

STUDENT PLAN   MELODY

(worksheet to be filled in by student teacher)

OBJECTIVES

to review contour, phrase, and sequence; to introduce pentatonic scale in songs and recordings; to use pentatonic ostinati in class

MATERIALS

STUDENT PLAN   MELODY
(student teacher worksheet, continued)

LESSON PLAN 3   RHYTHM

OBJECTIVES

to define/explore *beat* and *duple* and *triple meter*; to introduce *polymeter*

MATERIALS

"I've Been Working on the Railroad"
"Bridal March" from *Lohengrin*
"Star Spangled Banner"

ON THE BOARD

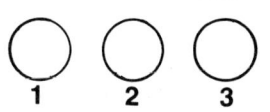

◯   ◯   ◯
1   2   3

Introduction

"How many of you have seen one of those medical shows on TV? Do you remember any of the scenes in intensive care or the operating room?" Draw, in the first circle, a simple sine wave ∼∼∼. "What would this tell us about the patient's pulse?" Draw, in the second circle, an erratic, jagged contour like ∿∧∨∿. "What about this patient?" Draw, in the last circle, a straight horizontal line _____. "What of this poor fellow?"

Content

"All music has some sort of a pulse, or beat. It may be even and regular, like #1, or irregular like #2. Sometimes the pulse in music is so faint it almost makes us feel as though the music were like #3. Notice that, with a person's pulse, there is a beat and then a pause or silence, like this:

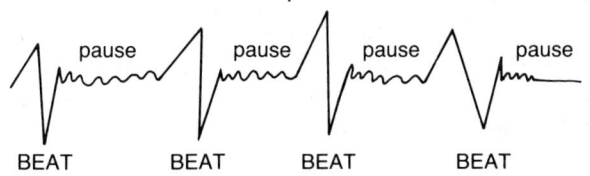

```
      pause        pause        pause        pause
   /\          /\           /\           /\
  /  \mmm    /  \mmm      /  \mmm      /  \___
 /    \/    /    \/      /    \/      /
BEAT        BEAT          BEAT         BEAT
```

"Musicians are interested in both the beat (or pulse) and what goes on during that pause in between. Take your own pulse." Allow time for this. "Let's discuss how our pulses might sound in words:

   Boom–shhh–boom–shhh–boom–shhh–boom–shhh. . . .

"See how this pulse becomes grouped into twos—**heavy**, light, **heavy**, light, etc. OR 1,2,1,2, etc. This grouping of strong with weak is called *meter* in music." Put term on board.

   Experiment with clapping beats organized into 1, 2; 1, 2, 3; and 1, 2, 3, 4. "When the pulse regularly moves 1, 2, 1, 2, we say the music moves in twos and call it *duple meter*." Put term on board. "Can you say your name in duple meter? Here's an example: *Reggie Jackson* becomes:"

Go around the class. Get verbal response, and have interesting names put on the board by the students. Adding a basic downbeat for the pulse, point to students randomly and have them say their names within the duple meter scheme. If you wish, join eight names and contrive a simple spoken round.

"The meter we're using is called duple. The name comes from the heavy–light beat pattern. But your names go on top of this meter and may not divide into 1–2–1–2. For example, a name like Andrea or Reginald or Cynthia would look like this: ♫ . This is the *rhythm* of the name." Put term on board. "*Meter* has to do with the basic heartbeat of a piece, while *rhythm* means the way the words or names or melody tones move above the meter. Let's see how this works with some songs in our books." Examine and sing some of the songs in duple meter in your series books. Students should be able to distinguish between meter and rhythm and to perform each. For example, if you choose something like "Little David, Play on Your Harp," students should demonstrate their comprehension as follows:

"Next, listen to these short pieces." Play these on the piano. "When I point to the word *meter* on the board, and after I have played the piece, I want you to clap the basic pulse. When I point to *rhythm*, clap the pattern of notes you hear in the melody."

"I've Been Working on the Railroad"
"Bridal March" from *Lohengrin*
"Star Spangled Banner"

"What was different about the last piece?" (It moved in threes, not twos.) "Who can suggest a term for the meter of music that moves in threes [triple]? Remember, duple was for twos.

"In triple meter, the basic heartbeat is still there, but during that pause after each beat there are *two* more very quiet pulses. If we spoke a pattern of triple meter using 'Boom' and 'shh,' how would it sound [Boom–shh–shh]?

Sample Lesson Plans   **103**

"Let's work with duple and triple meters. Slap your knees on 'one' and clap on 'two.' After we get that going, I'll say 'triple meter' and then you slap your knees once, but clap twice evenly. Be alert, for I'll change back and forth. The basic heartbeat will be the same all the time." Start slowly and gradually increase the tempo. This should be fun, not mechanical in execution. Consider calling out "men only" or "just the third row," in the manner of the game, "Simon says."

"What would happen if, instead of switching back and forth, we did duple and triple meters at the same time? Let's see. To make it simple, we'll keep our steady beat; all the boys will say the word 'Basketball' evenly over and over, while the girls will say 'Music.' Follow these patterns on the board:"

Boys: 3 ♩ ♩ ♩
      Bas - ket - ball

Girls: 2 ♩ ♩
      Mu - sic

(or use this)

Boys: 3 >♩ ♩ ♩ | >♩ ♩ ♩ | >♩ ♩ ♩ |

Girls: 2 >♩ ♩ | >♩ ♩ | >♩ ♩ | >♩ ♩ |

Select any words or names you wish. Add knee slap/clapping if you can. Point out how the BOOM, or downbeat, shifts. With a class that can do this, have them clap/snap/accent only the first or accented beat in each of their respective measures and think/feel the silences in between. Thus:

Boys: 3 ♩ 𝄽 𝄽 | ♩ 𝄽 𝄽 | ♩ 𝄽 𝄽 | ♩

Girls: 2 ♩ 𝄽 | ♩ 𝄽 | ♩ 𝄽 | ♩ 𝄽

"When we combine one meter with another—at the same time—we call it *polymeter*." Put term on board. "*Poly* means many. Most pieces you hear may not use polymeters, but some composers have found that using different meters at the same time in a piece creates a special feel or effect that's just what they want to produce. We'll do more with these later, but for now, let's return to simple meters.

"We'll work just with the meter that groups beats into twos.

Lesson Plan 3   Rhythm

What did we call that meter [duple]? On the board are eight rhythm patterns. As I point to each, while keeping a constant beat, clap each one twice. Watch out for the ones that start ahead of the beat."

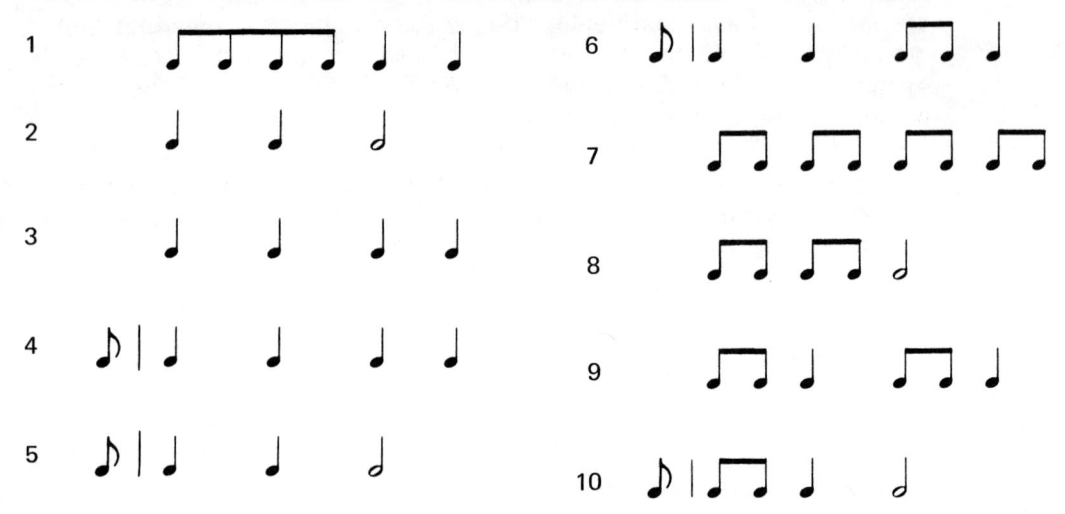

1 ♫♫ ♩ ♩
2 ♩ ♩ ♩
3 ♩ ♩ ♩ ♩
4 ♪|♩ ♩ ♩ ♩
5 ♪|♩ ♩ ♩
6 ♪|♩ ♩ ♫ ♩
7 ♫ ♫ ♫ ♫
8 ♫ ♫ ♩
9 ♫ ♩ ♫ ♩
10 ♪|♫ ♩ ♩

Next to these patterns, write the names of professional football teams or other sports teams:

Football Teams	
Cleveland Browns	San Francisco 49ers
Cincinnati Bengals	Kansas City Chiefs
Pittsburgh Steelers	New York Giants
Miami Dolphins	New York Jets
Green Bay Packers	Seattle Seahawks
Chicago Bears	Tampa Bay Buccaneers
Atlanta Falcons	San Diego Chargers
Oakland Raiders	Houston Oilers
New England Patriots	Dallas Cowboys
Minnesota Vikings	Los Angeles Rams

"Our game is this: Can you match team names to the correct numbered rhythm patterns you just did?" Talk through the rhythm of each team if necessary. Note the team names that begin with an upbeat. When the students can speak/clap the rhythms without much hesitation, here are some options for going on:

Option 1

Use just the names and make it a spoken canon, dividing into two or three groups. Erase some names to make it come out evenly.

Option 2

Keep the names, and have class chant the names to a steady beat. Let some volunteers provide a rhythmic background with brushes on cymbals:

cymbals ♩ ♫ ♩ ♫ ♩ ‖

Option 3

Erase the names and work only with the numbered rhythms. Clap/slap the rhythms within a steady beat.

Option 4

Assign a small group to represent each team named. Let the groups select classroom instruments to perform the rhythm of the name. By simply pointing to each team on the board—either in order or randomly—you can add the ingredient of varying tone color to this exercise. If this plan works well for you, return to it seasonally, varying the teams and sports accordingly.

Review

"Today we've worked with the idea of beat or pulse, meter, and rhythm. Let's see if you can demonstrate what you understand about them."
  Behaviors sought, individually and by group:

1. Clap a steady beat.
2. Clap an unsteady beat.
3. Stomp/clap a pattern of duple meter.
4. Stomp/clap a pattern of triple meter.
5. On a given song, show the difference between the beat and the rhythm of the melody.
6. Successfully perform team names with the appropriate rhythm.
7. Locate by page numbers duple- and triple-meter songs in the series books.
8. Aurally identify the meter of selected examples (records, tapes, or improvised by teacher) by circling or underlining the meter signature, as shown here:

    Example 1:   2/4   3/4   4/4

    Example 2:   2/4   3/4   4/4

STUDENT PLAN   RHYTHM

(worksheet to be filled in by student teacher)

OBJECTIVES

to review beat and meter; to introduce compound meter (6/8)

MATERIALS (suggested)

"He's a Jolly Good Fellow"
"Sumer is Icumen In"
"Seventy-six Trombones"
"Greensleeves"
"America" (*West Side Story*)

STUDENT PLAN   RHYTHM
(student teacher worksheet, continued)

LESSON PLAN 4 ORCHESTRATION FOR CLASSROOM INSTRUMENTS

OBJECTIVES

to develop an accompaniment to a given song; to investigate tone color

MATERIALS

piano, autoharp, tone bars, glockenspiel, bongos, triangle, guitar and/or string bass, recorders

This plan is different. It is intended to show how a whole variety of classroom instruments can be incorporated into the "orchestration" of a song in class. It is only one approach to arranging, and it can be applied to almost any song that might be selected for use. The harmonic analysis of a given song will determine the extent of the deviation from this plan. The song chosen here was selected because it

1. is easy to sing, though wide in range
2. uses only four chords
3. has a harmonic underpinning of I, VI, II, V^7 so common in many songs

"I Love the Mountains"[4]

Step 1: Do a harmonic analysis of the selected song. Except for the "tag ending," the harmonic scheme is simple and repetitive:

D: I   VI   II V^7 V^7 I

Step 2: Separate your available instruments into pitched and unpitched groups:

Pitched Instruments	Unpitched Instruments
piano	bongos
autoharp	triangle
tone bars	sticks
glockenspiel/xylophone	wood block
guitar	tambourine
string bass	cymbals
recorder, etc.	guiro, etc.

4. In Eisman, Jones, and Malone, *Making Music Your Own*, pp. 138–39.

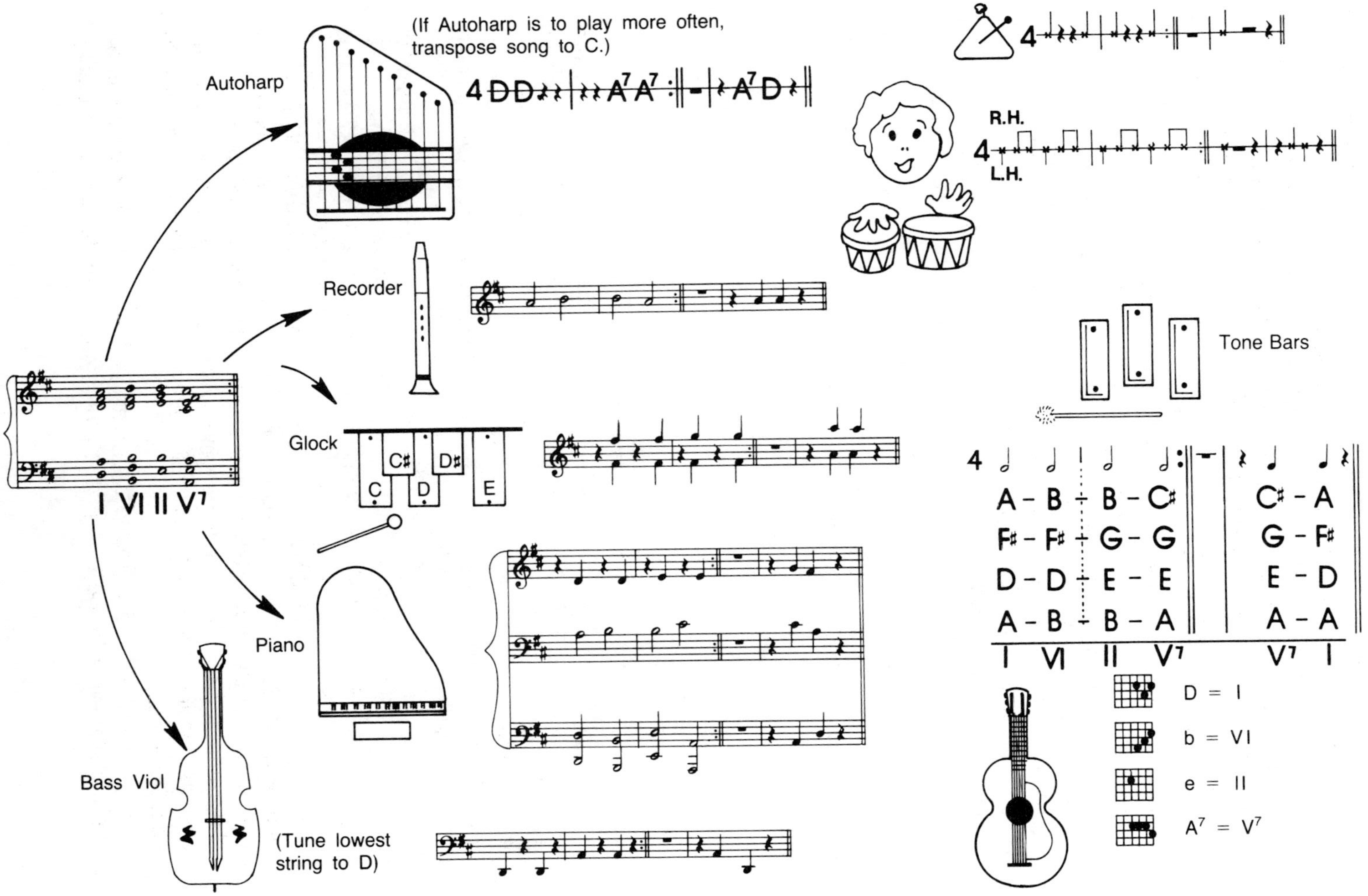
(If Autoharp is to play more often, transpose song to C.)
Autoharp
4 D D | A7 A7 :|| | A7 D
R.H.
L.H.
Recorder
Tone Bars
Glock
C C♯ D D♯ E
4
A – B B – C♯ C♯ – A
F♯ – F♯ G – G G – F♯
D – D E – E E – D
A – B B – A A – A
I VI II V7 V7 I
D = I
b = VI
e = II
A7 = V7
I VI II V7
Piano
Bass Viol
(Tune lowest string to D)

Step 3: Consider transposing the key, if melody range seems to dictate, or if guitar chords would be easier.

Step 4: Divide the harmonic motion from your analysis into separate, narrow melodic patterns, keeping in mind the unique performance problems of each instrument. Try to make the arrangement as easy as possible—you can always add complexity with a receptive, skillful class. Use any inversion or additional chord member to keep the line easy. Avoid fast changes, awkward leaps, and difficult guitar chords. Fit the arrangement to the playing needs of the class and the instruments.

Step 5: Rehearse briefly with each instrument or group of like instruments. Do not try it all at once. Consider working with pairs, such as bass and piano, or guitar and autoharp, or glockenspiel and tone bars. Get as many students involved in playing as possible. Demonstrate the correct manner of instrumental playing to all first (claves, for example, are usually gripped tightly in both fists, with no resultant resonance). Switch personnel frequently—do not let Jane play bass the whole time.

Step 6: Add voices for the melodic line and go through the song. Practice the ending first, using all pitched instruments on the perfect final cadence. Then, add the voices with the following:

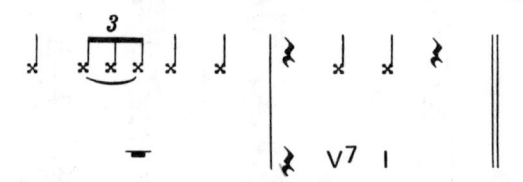

Step 7: Once a reasonable ensemble performance can be achieved, discuss the importance of dynamics and choice of instruments. Are some sounds inappropriate to the text/mood of the song? What could be substituted? Could the entire instrumental ensemble play pianissimo? Should the dynamic level increase as the melody ascends? Discuss and *perform* any musical suggestions made by the class. Do not permit a solely verbal response to answer the ideas suggested in class.

Step 8: A. Consider the idea of numbering each instrument or instrumental group. For example, we might call the bass #1, piano #2, autoharp #3, glockenspiel #4, recorder #5, guitar #6, tone bars #7, bongos #8, and triangle #9. With a responsive class, you might wish to add the ingredient of unpredictability into the performance. Calling out, "Only even numbers" or "Numbers 4 through 9 only" is not so much a musical choice (though it certainly could be) as it is one way to have some fun with such classroom orchestrations. In the beginning, make the actual performance as easy as possible. Skip theoretical explanations until there is a demonstrated need to know.

B. Feel free to alter tunings, if it helps. Scordatura can be applied effectively to the string bass (open strings are far easier to pluck).

Guitar chording is not easy for tender fingers. In a song that uses only all major or all minor chords, the guitar can be altered as follows:

Using a heavy Hawaiian-guitar bar (or a smooth, round pencil or something else flat and smooth), one can slide up and down the fingerboard to change the chord. Avoid excessive scordatura. Let a step and one-half be the limit for any upward alteration of a string. The glissando effect in chord changes lends itself well to any pop or country/Western song. Let the guitar lie flat on one's lap or on a desk. Further, using the mother-of-pearl (or metal) dots that are inlaid within the fingerboard can help the younger player quickly find the commonly used chords.

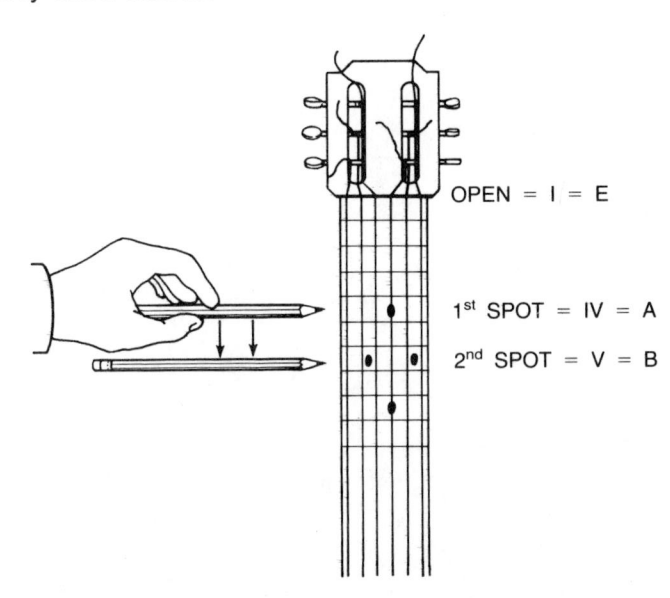

OPEN = I = E

1st SPOT = IV = A

2nd SPOT = V = B

   C. Incorporating the piano and autoharp (and bass and guitar) can be made simpler with the use of colored tape. If students have trouble coordinating eyes and hands on the autoharp, it is helpful to put a small square of colored tape (or use masking tape colored over) on the chord bars. You can then simplify the effort by saying, "Play two reds, one yellow, and a blue." The piano keyboard can be coded the same way. Remember, the rule is first to get your students *performing,* whatever it takes. Once confidence is built and success occurs frequently, then ease away from these techniques. Too many lessons are lost because the students lack the knowledge, insight, strength, or coordination that the teacher assumes the students have.

    D. Not every song merits this sort of wholesale orchestration. Be selective; when appropriate, suggest classroom instruments that are clearly out of place to test pupils' sensitivity to tone color. Do not use the guiro or triangle with *every* song you do. Encourage the class to listen, judge, and choose. Once a song orchestration has been completed, consider playing for the class the record arrangement available in the record set that accompanies the series book. Do this after, not before, their performance in class. Is the students' interpretation better? Mention text, mood, quality, and so on.

STUDENT PLAN   **ORCHESTRATION FOR CLASSROOM INSTRUMENTS**

(worksheet to be filled in by student teacher)

OBJECTIVES	MATERIALS
to develop an accompaniment to a given song; to explain and use I, IV, and V chords	tone bars, xylophones, keyboard

STUDENT PLAN   ORCHESTRATION FOR CLASSROOM INSTRUMENTS

(student teacher worksheet, continued)

Sample Lesson Plans   115

LESSON PLAN 5   RHYTHM
(perhaps several days)

OBJECTIVES
to define and explore *ostinato* as a repetitive device in melody and in rhythm

MATERIALS
blank paper

ON THE BOARD

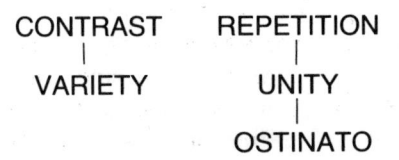

CONTRAST   REPETITION
  | |
VARIETY   UNITY
               |
             OSTINATO

Introduction

(Assign two readers to this.)

#1
"Railroads are neat. Riding on a train is a great experience. You should all ride a train sometime."

#2
(begins and ends alone)

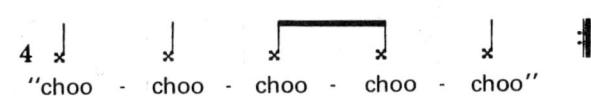

"choo - choo - choo - choo - choo"

(repeated over and over)

Here's another:
"Railroads are neat" (said the same over and over). Begins and ends alone.

(woodblock or sticks)

Content

"You heard two short demonstrations. What stayed the same in the first one ['choo-choo,' or rhythm]? What about the second [the verse or the words]? What word do we think of when we say something goes on the same over and over? We say it _____ [repeats]. *Repetition* [point to word on board] is very important in our lives and in art. Our lives have many kinds of repetition. We awake, have something to eat, go to school or to our work, have a lunch break, go back to school or to work, have supper, relax or do homework, sleep, then get up again. Repeating things is important in every part of our lives. Even our faces are well organized with two eyes, two ears, a nose, and a mouth. Yet we all look and act differently. We do different things, like different foods, enjoy different sports, drive different cars. We are all the *same* in that we all breathe, eat, drink, live and die, but we are all *different* because we do these things in our own special way. Your life has both *unity* with the lives of others and *variety* because each one of you is unique.

"Art has the same things. We like to see and hear patterns [unity] and yet enjoy something else to break the monotony [variety]. Today we will work with one of the most important parts in all art—*unity*, as we see it in art and hear it in music.

"Let's see if you understand what I mean about *repetition*. We will try to make some designs that repeat over and over."

On the board, draw a large square with chalk. In that enclosed area, draw a simple pattern, such as

⬜ or ⬜ or ⬜.

Get students to come forward and complete your idea by repeating it. Encourage using the whole space, but keep it simple at first.

"Some of this looks like a design we might see—where in your home [wallpaper, wall molding, book edges, kitchen tile, etc.]? Designs like this are very repetitious—they seem solid and strong because they repeat one idea over and over. Music uses this same idea. Repeating a musical idea is like cement—it keeps all the musical bricks from falling down. Repetition makes a piece stronger.

"Let's see if we can find repetition in some music you know. Listen and tell me what stays the same over and over." Select a song in your series, or from the current popular repertoire, or from TV commercials. Search for simple bass ostinati, or chord progressions, or melodic motifs that repeat consistently. Investigate what it is that repeats in each of your selections.

"We have a special word in music for things that repeat over and over. We say such a part is an *ostinato*. [Point to *ostinato* on the board.] Can anyone think of another word that looks and sounds like *ostinato* and means the same thing ['obstinate']? Obstinate, ostinato—stubborn; it won't change, no matter what. What parts of music, or which elements [like rhythm or melody], can stay the same throughout a piece?" Try to lead the class to realize that *anything* audible can be an ostinato. "Usually, we think of a rhythm that goes on over and over, or a short melody that repeats. Do not limit yourself to these, but usually when we speak of an ostinato we mean either rhythm or melody. Let's see how good your ears are. Listen to these and tell me if the ostinato is rhythmic or melodic:

Rhythmic

Melodic

(vary the rhythm)

Both

"All right, let's see if you really understand ostinato. Carla, come down and make up an ostinato pattern on the drum." It could be as simple as the following:

So accept anything that demonstrates an understanding. If this was correct for a rhythmic ostinato, continue: "Troy, come down and make up a melodic ostinato." Supply some tone bars or a limited span on the piano keyboard. Continue until he demonstrates the idea.

"Usually, if an ostinato is played on a tone-producing instrument, it will be both rhythmic and a melodic. Here is a familiar bass line to many songs you know. It is both a rhythmic and a melodic ostinato:

I   VI   II   V

"Who can give us a definition of ostinato? Could there be a harmonic ostinato, where the same chords repeat over and over? Would that be an ostinato?

"Now, even with wallpaper and floor tile, you will want to have some variety, some change of pace. A tune that never changes—that is, an ostinato—may not be very rewarding. So, to the unity given by an ostinato, we usually add something different to balance it, like this:

Lesson Plan 5   Rhythm

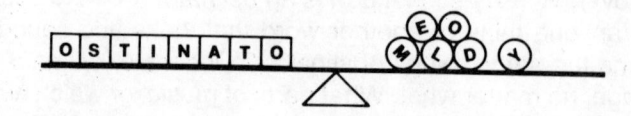

"*Unity* and *variety* are key words in all art. Patterns that repeat in music give strength and unity; changes and contrast give us variety within that same unity.

"Here's today's musical problem. I want four groups." Divide by row or line, to come up with four approximately equal groups. Divide all available classroom instruments among them, and use the corners of the room. "Your task will be to create some ostinati that will go with a song in our series book." Select a short, easy tune with simple harmonic structure.

"First, let's review the song." Sing it without any accompaniment or interpretation. "Now, that's the song I want you to keep in mind. Look at the words, the speed, the key, the chord symbols, and so forth. Then get together in your groups and experiment with the instruments I've provided. Create your own rhythmic and melodic ostinati. If you can write them down, fine. Try to have as many of you playing as possible. Each group will perform its work for the rest of the class, and we will comment on your performance. I will signal you when your time is up."

Split up instruments and groups, circulate, and help only if necessary. Give the groups a few minutes to explore the instruments and to select the patterns they want. What you seek is a demonstration that they understand what *ostinato* means and can create one to a simple song.

Let other students comment on the performances. You play the piece on the piano with each group. Keep in mind the patterns that seem particularly well constructed. You may wish to combine them again later.

If you have a slide projector or art books available, consider showing the class works by Bridget Riley (*Current*), Franz Marc (*Tower of Blue Horses*), or Hans Hartung (*The Whirlwind*) for examples of repetition. For both unity and variety, discuss the pictures in *Silver Burdett Music, Grade 7; Sound, Beat, and Feeling;* or the reproductions available in the series in your school. Help pupils note (*a*) repetitions of color, line, shape, and texture; and (*b*) aspects that offer contrast. For an additional musical example, use Bizet's L'Arlesienne Suite No. 1 ("Carillon").

Review

"Now to conclude our work today. Let's see if you can remember what we did and said today. I would like to see these when you're finished, so put your names on these papers." Pass out blank paper. Number the items 1 to 7. "Finish these sentences:

1. A rhythmic ostinato is a _____.

2. A melodic ostinato is a _____.

3. Repetition in art gives us _____.

4. Contrast in art gives us _____."

Listening examples—use **R** (rhythm ostinato), **M** (melodic ostinato), **B** (both):

5. [musical notation in bass clef]

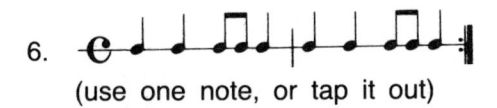

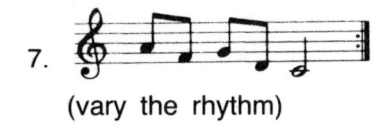

6. [musical notation]
   (use one note, or tap it out)

7. [musical notation in treble clef]
   (vary the rhythm)

STUDENT PLAN   RHYTHM

(worksheet to be filled in by student teacher)

OBJECTIVES **MATERIALS** **ON THE BOARD**

to define and explore *ostinato* further

STUDENT PLAN   RHYTHM
(student teacher worksheet, continued)

LESSON PLAN 6   RHYTHM, DYNAMICS, TONE COLOR

OBJECTIVES

to introduce the spoken fugue; to explore words, dynamics, and the importance of instrumental color; to review rhythms to include the triplet

MATERIALS

usual classroom instruments, ditto of text shown below, copies of the spoken fugue

Introduction

"Tell me the first word that comes to your mind when I say 'ice cream' _____ [cone, sundae, social, dessert, etc.]; 'left' _____ [out, handed, cross, jab, right, side, etc.]; 'caboose' _____ [train, railroad, choo-choo, etc.]; or 'tracks' _____ [similar terms]."

Content

"Today we will work with the idea of railroad trains—how they go and how they sound—and we'll make it all musical. Last time we began class with two demonstrations with words and rhythms, that led to our discussion of ostinato. What did we decide an 'ostinato' was?" (Response.)

"We will use some ostinati today, but first let's look at these words [read the text with the class aloud]:

> Here comes the train,
> It's rolling down the track
> Listen to all of those wheels
> Go clickety, clickety, clack——It's
> Puffing——hissing——ss!——ff!
> Now it's coming nearer, closer, louder.
> Ding, ding, ding, ding——
> Here's the engine, here's a coal car,
> Here's a box car, here's a flat car,
> Here come 500 Volkswagens,
> There went the train
> It's rolling down the track!

"The words are easy. They describe the sight and sound of a train. But we need to do more than just read them. Who can read these words so that they really paint a clear picture? Make your voice match the words and feelings about trains." Get several volunteers and withhold comment until several have tried. Let us assume some students have caught the idea, with appropriate inflection and dynamics. "Where is the train when we started reading the words? Where is it in the middle of the text? At the conclusion? What does the distance suggest for how our voices should be as we read? Should we read each line the same? Where would we say the words the loudest? The softest? What should happen to the volume of our voices in between?" Work to an understanding of appropriate overall dynamics.

Put on board: <♢>

"If I asked some of you to create an ostinato of just a few of the text's words only, which words would you select? Why?" Try out any suggestions.

"If some of you read the words and others had to make musical sounds on our classroom instruments to go with the words, which instruments would you select? Why? What patterns or ostinati might suggest the sound of the train?" Again, let volunteers select and perform for class critique.

"Now, we will put all of this together—readers on words, readers with word ostinati, and other students playing ostinati on instruments. Remember the *dynamics* [point to <♢> on the board]." Assign one drum player to maintain a steady, even beat throughout. Comment on the quality of the students' performance. Ask if they felt they created the sounds and feelings of moving trains.

Put on the board, or have prepared, these patterns:

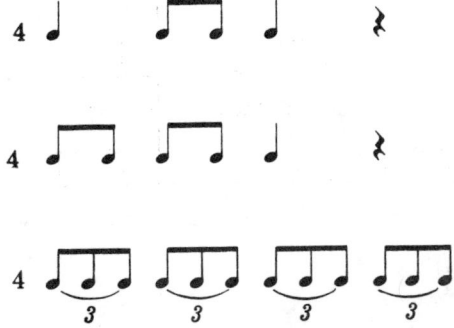

[musical notation: 4/4 quarter, two eighths quarter, quarter, quarter rest]

[musical notation: 4/4 two eighths, two eighths, quarter, quarter rest]

[musical notation: 4/4 four triplets]

"We will return to these words soon, but let's do something else now. Here are three rhythm patterns [point to board]. Clap each line until I tell you to switch to another." Rehearse each line. The triplet will present problems for some. Be prepared to help. Ultimately you want to be able to point randomly from one line to another and have them clap without breaking the basic pulse.

"From the words we just used, where would the triplet figure fit best? What about the first pattern? The second? Let's try two patterns together." Divide class in half; one group does "clickety" over and over; the second group does "rolling down the track." Divide the first group in half; one group continues the triplet pattern while the other adds "here comes the train." When stable, add the other half of the class so that the three patterns

124 Lesson Plan 6   Rhythm, Dynamics, Tone Color

FIGURE 7.1 *Spoken Fugue*

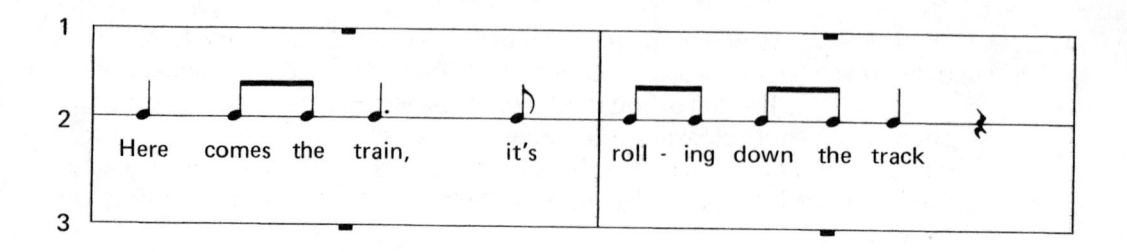

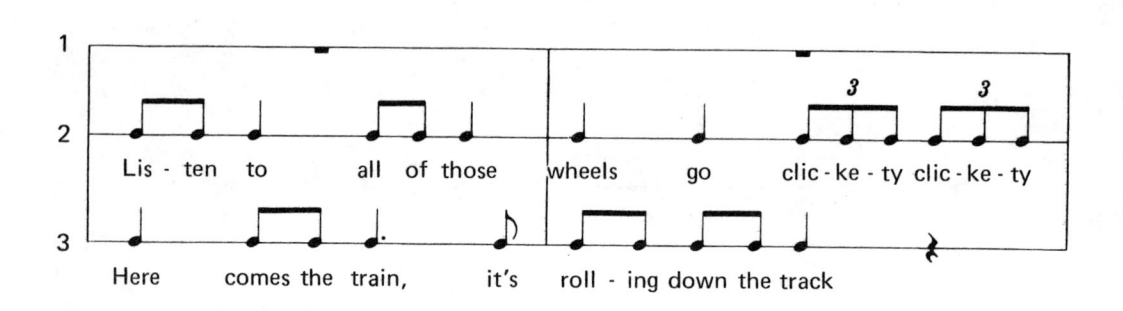

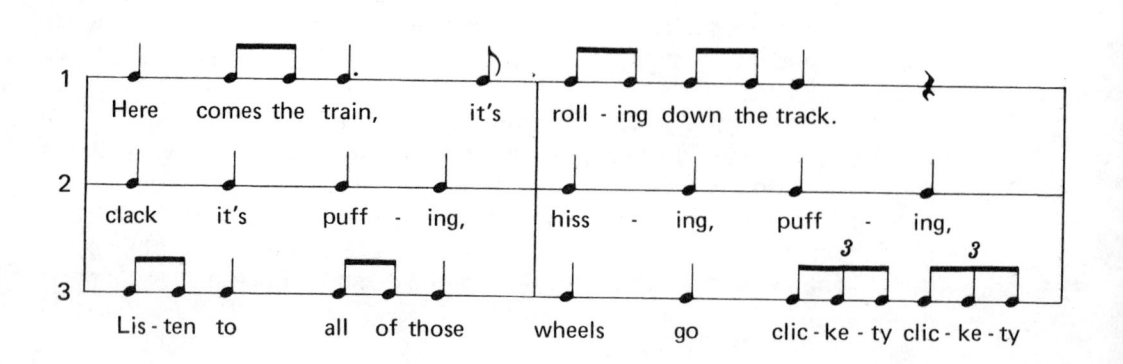

Sample Lesson Plans   **125**

Line 1: Now it's com-ing near - er | clos - er loud - er
Line 2: hiss - ing, hiss - ing, | hiss - ing, hiss - ing
Line 3: clack, ding ding | ding ding ding

Line 1: ding ding ding ding ding ding ding ding | ding ding ding ding ding ding ding ding
Line 2: SS! FF! SS! FF! | SS! FF! SS! FF!
Line 3: clic-ke-ty clic-ke-ty clic-ke-ty clic-ke-ty | clic-ke-ty clic-ke-ty clic-ke-ty clic-ke-ty

Line 1: ding ding ding ding, Here comes the | train, it's roll-ing down the
Line 2: Here comes the train, it's | roll-ing down the track, Here's the
Line 3: clic-ke-ty clic-ke-ty clic-ke-ty clic-ke-ty, Here | comes the train, it's

Line 1: track   ding ding ding ding | SS! SS! ding ding ding ding
Line 2: en - gine, here's a coal | car, here's a box car,
Line 3: roll-ing down the track, | ding ding ding ding, SS! SS!

126 Lesson Plan 6 Rhythm, Dynamics, Tone Color

1: SS! SS! ding ding ding ding | SS! ding ding SS! ding ding
2: here's a flat car, here come | five hun-dred Volks - wa - gens
3: ding ding ding ding SS! SS! | ding ding SS! ding ding SS!

1: There went the | train, it's roll-ing down the
2: There went the train, it's | roll-ing down the track, it's
3: There went the | train, it's

1: track, it's roll-ing down the | track, it's roll-ing down the
2: roll-ing down the track, it's | roll-ing down the track, it's
3: roll - ing down the | track, Lis-ten to

Repeat and fade

1: track, it's roll-ing down the | track, it's roll-ing down the
2: roll-ing down the track, it's | roll-ing down the track, it's
3: all of those wheels go | clic-ke-ty clic-ke-ty clic-ke-ty clic-ke-ty

combine. Have a student conductor lead the class and, by pointing from group to group, emphasize the dynamic level of each group's pattern.

"All of this work is to make our next job easier. The words and patterns we have been using were put together into a short piece called a speaking *fugue*." Put the term on the board. "After we have worked with this piece, I'll ask you for ideas about what a fugue might mean. Keep in your same three groups."

Spread the groups out in class, if possible. Explain the nature of the notation—that is, explain why a musical staff is not necessary. Point out that the lines are numbered, and that each group has a specific line assigned to it. You may wish to rehearse the lines separately.

Let the size and ability of each class determine your procedure. Try to get through the piece without being too picky. Keep a steady beat going, working for rhythmic stability first. Then review what the students did earlier with dynamics <>, articulation, accents, etc. Once the piece can be done reasonably well in three parts, your options are many:

1. Tape-record the students' performance and ask them to critique it.
2. Repeat performance but add simple instrumental ostinati as desired.
3. Reduce the spoken portion to one or two lines and substitute a wholly instrumental rendition of the other part(s).
4. With a very small class, have all students do line 1 and tape-record it. Then, on the playback, have parts 2 and 3 be performed live.
5. Use instruments only on "descriptive" words—"puffing," "ding-ding," "ss," and the like.
6. Consider introducing a "sprechtstimme" quality by encouraging parts to alter the pitch as they perform.
7. Divide each of the three groups into three groups. Then have each group compete to produce the most accurate, most inventive rendition.

"Look over the piece a moment. I said it was a kind of *fugue* [point to term on the board]. What about the way this piece is put together—not the <> but the patterns?" Try to get the students to notice (*a*) the gradual entry of voices; (*b*) the repetition of rhythm patterns; (*c*) the way voices enter in m. 11–12 compared to m. 1–5; (*d*) the shift in accent in part 2, m. 12–16; (*e*) the augmentation in part 3, m. 17–20. "We will look at other pieces in fugal form later. Keep in mind these features that we just discussed." Jot the accurate observations on the board and point to them.

Lesson Plan 6   Rhythm, Dynamics, Tone Color

Review

"You noticed that the words and rhythms paint a good picture of trains. The dynamics we used made good sense. If we had kept the volume the same throughout, would the effect have been as good? What about accents? Did they help? Is the selection of appropriate instruments important? We have explored *dynamics, tone color,* and *fugal form* today on our train trip."[5]

---

5. For substitutes or additional musical material relating to either trains or < >, see the following:

"Rock Island Line," "Casey Jones" (traditional); "Nine Hundred Miles" (Eisman, Jones, and Malone, *Making Music Your Own, Grade 8*, p. 185); "This Train" (Choate et al., *Sound, Beat, and Feeling, Grade 7*, p. 138); "New River Train" (Reimer et al., *Silver Burdett Music, Grade 7*, p. 87); "A Spoken Fugue" (Eisman, Jones, and Malone, *Making Music Your Own, Grade 7*, p. 54); "Original Talking Blues" (Marsh et al., *Spectrum of Music, Grade 6*, p. 129); "The Little Train of the Caipira" from Bachianas Brasileiras No. 2 by Villa-Lobos; "Pacific 231" by Honegger; and "Fêtes" from Nocturnes by Debussy.

STUDENT PLAN   RHYTHM, DYNAMICS, TONE COLOR

(worksheet to be filled in by student teacher)

OBJECTIVES

to review the spoken fugue; to explore the words, dynamics, and instrumental color of a new spoken fugue; to reinforce this work with a short listening lesson

MATERIALS

STUDENT PLAN   RHYTHM, DYNAMICS, TONE COLOR

(student teacher worksheet, continued)

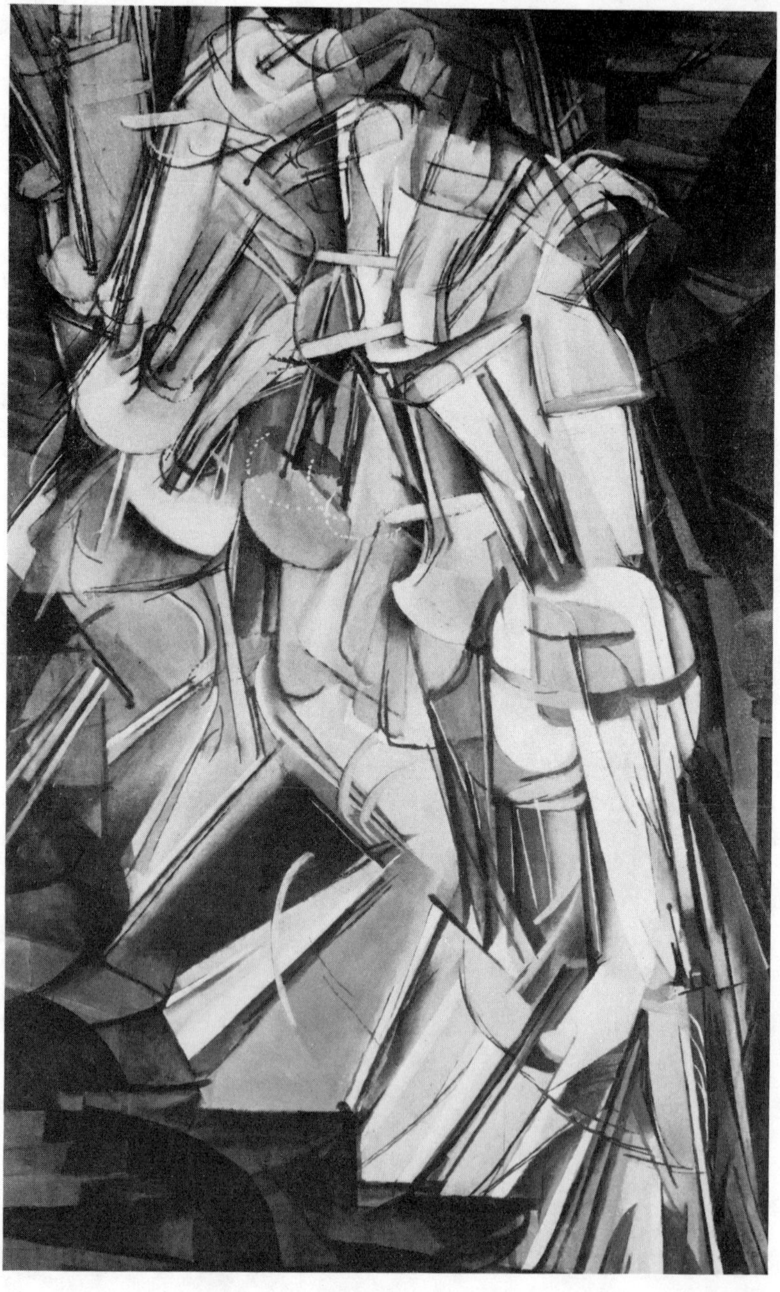

It's clever, but is it art?

Rudyard Kipling

The Allied Arts

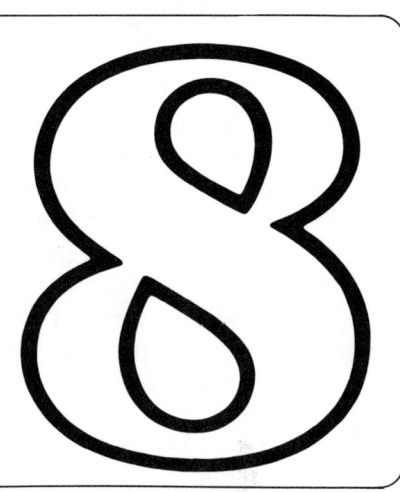

8

The middle school general music curriculum *in practice* has remained relatively stable over the past decades. Yet recent trends have blossomed and have become well established in the overall content and administration of today's general music. Mention has already been made about the role of popular music. To this, we can add a growing awareness of non-Western music; contracts and individualization; and certainly, the growing interest in the allied arts.

By "allied arts" we mean the fine arts—for example, music, painting, sculpture, dance, architecture, and literature. This arrangement should not be confused with the "humanities," which in addition include ethics, philosophy, and history. Many schools and publishers state that they promote or publish humanities-oriented classes and products. "Humanities" means different things to different people, however. Our concern will be the fine arts (allied arts) and how they may be incorporated into the middle school music program.

The degree of difficulty in implementing any allied arts program is related directly to how thoroughly one wishes to research and explore the various approaches. The vast resources available for allied arts (texts, curricula, modules, films, museums, to mention only a few) may leave one feeling overwhelmed. Further, the novice encounters many conflicting points of view from qualified writers.

Let us examine briefly one source of this lack of consensus. Just as we noted the differences among the formalists, referentialists, and expressionists, now we may touch on the contrasting views of the "purists" and the "confederates." Purists state that one cannot really combine the arts at all—that to do so violates the unique essence of each form of art. Purists feel that no two arts are, in any sense, similar; their materials and techniques are too different. Further, no two arts develop equally. A vocabulary that serves all of the arts equally well does not exist. The best one can do, the purists feel, is to study each art individually.

Those who adopt such a point of view obviously see no need for an allied arts approach. Their contribution to our investigation, however, is in no way minimal. By making us aware of the perils of teaching relationships among the arts, the purists lead us to be cautious and insightful about our approach. Surely, the intelligent teacher is aware that there are basic artistic problems in attempting to compare a Rubens canvas with a Bach organ work. To explain them as equivalent is not only misleading but also actually incorrect.

Reimer's Flow Chart

The final chapter of Reimer's *A Philosophy of Music Education* concerns itself with approaches to the allied arts. Reimer concludes that most of the traditional approaches are weakened by their extra-artistic organization. Concluding his review, he suggests the model shown in Figure 8.1. The individual roles are shown at the top. The largest box indicates that the "formula" for the aesthetic experience—perception ←→ reaction—is applicable to all three roles (creator, re-creator, and experiencer). The smaller boxes to the left and right identify additional dimensions common to all the arts. The final box, at the bottom, represents the specific art work. However, although the arrows seem to indicate that one should approach art study from the top row and proceed downward to the individual work, this may not be exactly what Reimer had in mind. If one accepts the idea that all the boxes are common dimensions, one could begin with any box. It is not necessary to always begin with the "creator" or the "experiencer"—in fact, to do so might lock our allied arts approach into unnecessary rigidity.

The strength of this model lies in its objectivity and its recognition of the variety of forces that shape every art work. It does not suggest that there is a common vocabulary among the arts, nor does it include instructions for the reaction component (for example, "Right, Bill, that was really sad music."). By excluding any interpretive component from this chart, Reimer avoids the need to confront those questions usually posed in nonaesthetic approaches ("What does it mean? What is it about? Is it happy or sad? Is this where the broom dances?").

The Allied Arts   135

FIGURE 8.1 *A Model for Generating Units of Instruction in General Aesthetic Education*

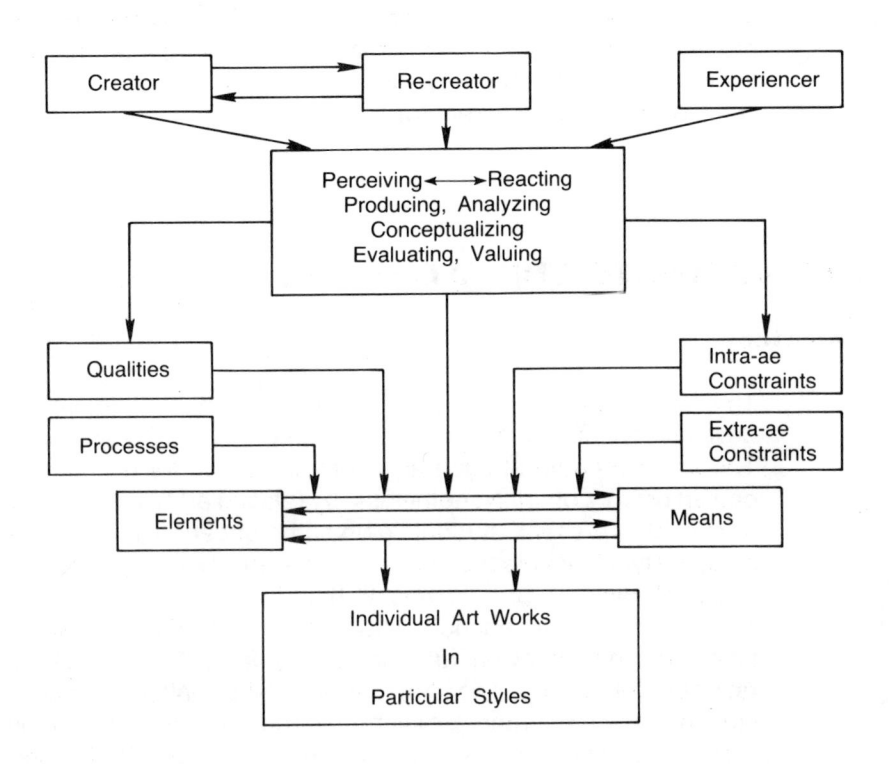

```
    Creator  ⇄  Re-creator              Experiencer
         ↘        ↓        ↙
         Perceiving ⇄ Reacting
         Producing, Analyzing
            Conceptualizing
          Evaluating, Valuing

    Qualities                          Intra-ae
                                       Constraints
    Processes                          Extra-ae
                                       Constraints
    Elements  ⇄⇄⇄  Means

         Individual Art Works
                  In
            Particular Styles
```

Source: Bennett Reimer, *A Philosophy of Music Education*, © 1970, p. 158. Reprinted by permission of Prentice-Hall, Inc., Englewood Cliffs, New Jersey.
boxed words = common dimensions among the arts
AE = aesthetic

Critics might point out various shortcomings or oversights in Figure 8.1, but one of the most immediate concerns is that it really does not help in planning an allied arts lesson. While certain dimensions are shown to be common to all the arts, the chart does not say anything about how one is to combine the arts. Rather, it indicates that such comparisons are inappropriate—that one may examine a particular work from different vantage points (constraints, elements, means, etc.), but one should not try to examine it with respect to other works. Thus, the chart implies that one should not ally the arts but should focus on the uniqueness of each artistic medium.

We are *music* educators first and foremost. However, we should recognize that the other fine arts may help us by appealing to the infinite variety of individual tastes and may actually boost our effectiveness as music teachers. If we agree that the arts *can* be used together, in some fashion, in lessons dealing with aesthetic education, then our interest turns to those approaches that show how arts can be combined. The "confederates" display a notable range of approaches. Let us now briefly discuss some of these approaches taken by allied arts practitioners, noting possible shortcomings as well as strengths.

APPROACHES TO THE ALLIED ARTS

Historical

This approach may well be the most common. It attempts to trace the development of all the arts under the umbrella of Western civilization history. The sheer breadth of such an approach allows for only superficial study of one art or work of art. Nonetheless, by relating art to the different time periods from past to present, students gain some understanding of when and where certain styles developed. One might justifiably call a course so directed "Cultural History" or "Art and History."

Some teachers who favor the historical idea simply reverse the time direction, studying art and history from "now" back to "then." The rationale for doing so is that current styles and events are close to the students' own reference, making Warhol or Penderecki more compelling than the Lascaux caves and tribal drum tattoos. Again, breadth and the problem of always having to present trends backwards pose large problems. Both types of historical approach tend to emphasize history rather than aesthetics. In fact, the historical approach—like any approach poorly implemented—can become totally devoid of arts content.

Sociological: *Zeitgeist*

This approach, in a basically historical perspective, uses the arts as "proof" of cultural and societal currents throughout history. The art of a given period is seen to reflect the conditions, emphases, and constraints of a particular society or culture. Art works are included to support sociological contentions. Examples are many: the societal unrest in late eighteenth-century France reflected in the canvases of David; the nineteenth-century escapism pursued by the Lake poets; Baroque splendor in rural German churches; Medieval piety in Cimabue; modern unrest with LeRoi Jones (Imamu Amiri Baraka).

While the historical tie-up with art is helpful in general, the selection of art examples usually is limited to only those works which clearly convey the feelings and pressures that the advocates define as salient features of a period. Often one speaks of such an approach as "self-fulfilling prophecy"— that is, characterize a period (for example, the Baroque) as lively, dynamic, restless, and then select art works that make that point. *Selection* is crucial here; one would search for those works of Rubens, Bernini, Dryden, and Bach that are lively, dynamic, and restless, "overlooking" the rest.

Despite the influence of TV and other media, today's middle school students are not as worldly and historically knowledgeable as some writers would have us believe. Further, middle school students usually take only American history, not the whole of Western civilization. If an allied arts course could provide even a "bare bones" historical framework, it would be more than many seventh and eighth graders now receive. But our primary concern is increasing students' sensitivity to the artistic aspects of life. A *Zeitgeist* approach is historical/cultural in focus, not aesthetic. The selectivity in this approach is very restrictive, and selected works tend to be discussed and interpreted in nonartistic ways.

"Man and _____"

Such a title frequently is seen in materials advertised in the "humanities" category.[1] The relation between "Man and Nature," "Man and Democracy," "Man and God," and so on is demonstrated, again, by the selection of art works. Literary works especially are treated in this sort of organization. In Connolly's collection, this strategy is evident.[2] The table of contents includes this:

> I. What is Man?
> The Beginning of Awareness
> The Heroic Image
> The Tragic Experience
> The Comic Experience
> Thought and Language
> II. What is Man's Measure?
> The Measure of Excellence
> The Measure of Love
> The Measure of Justice
> The Measure of Wisdom

---

1. The use of the term *man* in the generic sense is no longer considered appropriate by many people. These materials do, however, use the term in this way.
2. Francis Connolly, *Man and His Measure* (New York: Harcourt, Brace and World, 1964), pp. vii–xvi.

Examples of prose and poetry are arranged around these categories. While the selection itself is remarkable and praiseworthy, this fine collection is not designed as a practical vehicle for teaching aesthetics. The book is simply a splendid anthology of literature.

So far, this discussion has noted briefly some of the frequently encountered approaches that select and order artistic endeavors past and present as they fit into nonaesthetic frameworks. While these strategies may be useful to teachers, they may well miss the points aesthetic educators continually emphasize—namely, that good and great art can be appreciated without regard to when or where it was done; that such art is timeless; and that through skillful presentation and analysis, art can promote increased sensitivity to and insight about the whole world of feeling. Let us now examine approaches which seem directed to purely artistic concerns.

Exemplars

We may define an *exemplar* as something worthy of imitation—a model; in art, a creation acknowledged by experts as outstanding or significant. Advocates of turning only to exemplars favor a program in which a limited number of "classics" are studied in depth. The Yale Report suggested such a scheme in music:[3] Students would bypass breadth in favor of depth, studying one concerto, one ballet, one opera, and so on—"better a few well than many superficially." For help in selecting works for study, one must turn to the connoisseur for expert judgment.

Every facet of the art world has its body of exemplars, works proven by time and scrutiny and worthy of inclusion into an artistic Valhalla: the Parthenon, the viaduct at Pont du Gard, Chartres, Giotto's Padua frescos, the Sistine Chapel ceiling, the Mona Lisa, the B minor Mass, *Hamlet*. Such works become the content of the curriculum, to be probed with regard to aesthetics, history, and culture. The main focus is artistic, though providing for the additional insight gained from areas not directly related to art. Thus, in studying, say, *Petrouchka*, one not only listens to the whole work but also examines the full score, investigates the story, and reads of staging and costumery.

That the exemplar approach is oriented toward aesthetics is most commendable. However, middle school students need variety and a fast pace. While some academically gifted students might enjoy a class with

---

3. Joseph Turner, "Innovation and Experiment in Music Education," *Council for Research in Music Education* Bulletin No. 6 (Fall 1965): 1–8; also Kenneth L. Wendrich, "An Approach to Musical Understanding for Secondary School Students," ibid: 9–11.

intense, singular concentration, most general music students probably would not. Therefore, the exemplar approach, though worthy of consideration for special classes, may not suit the needs of most music classes. If certain art works do stir the class' interest and concentration, the teacher surely should provide every opportunity for deeper investigation and analysis. Teachers need to be sensitive to sudden spurts of class interest; they can occur in the most unlikely places and times. This author recalls vividly the interest in an eighth-grade music class during a casual discussion of the architecture and symbolism of Notre Dame (Paris).

Subject Matter

In the search for good arrangements of various art works, teachers often select this strategy. Course content is organized around frequently encountered genres, such as the landscape, the free-standing sculpture, the portrait, the geometric, the Nativity, the Crucifixion, the Resurrection, or the social comment. Thus, teachers can select art works whose title or major emphasis is clear enough to allow for categorization. Further, teachers who take this approach often provide variety by comparing and contrasting numerous works similarly titled or intended. A class may be asked to deal with three interpretations of the Crucifixion—by Grunewald, Rubens, and Dali. Or the class may compare a wooden German Baroque crucifix and a painting. Or, as Dudley and Faricy suggest, they could compare Brueghel's *Fall of Icarus* with a poem by Auden.[4] The cement is the subject matter, not the materials or media. As a result, one can jump from one area of artistic production to another by noting the similarities and differences among several works dealing with the same topic.

One might argue that *any* curricular arrangement that introduces a nonaesthetic dimension (subject matter) should be rejected. But this approach should not be dismissed lightly. The good teacher recognizes the value of having a logical and practical organization that can provide opportunities for aesthetic growth. *Selection* is crucial: Which topics or subject matter will one choose? Just as important, which topics will be excluded?

The basic problem with this approach, aside from its restrictive selectivity, is that the skills and insights gained may not apply to the great variety of art works one may encounter in life. Students should be equipped with the experiences and techniques to deal with any art work, regardless of its date or where it was created.

In contrast, subject matter advocates believe that students need some anchoring in the past—a sense of how artists have dealt with

---

4. Louise Dudley and Austin Faricy, *Humanities*, 4th ed. (New York: McGraw-Hill Book Company, 1967).

recurrent problems or subjects. Students cannot have this background if the allied arts program is structured around the ability to cope with continuous change (or "future shock"). As we shall see, perhaps the best solution lies somewhere in the middle.

Artistic Elements

Every art has its unique essential elements. In music, we think of elements as being melody, rhythm, harmony, texture, tone color, and form. In the visual arts, we speak of line, shape, texture, value, color, space, and mass. Thus, elements—or ingredients—are different from "principles," such as repetition, variation, and so on. By dealing primarily with the arrangement and use of elements in a given art work, we can analyze and discuss them in a rather impersonal, objective manner. We can avoid any personal involvement with "What does this mean?" or "Is this a happy or a sad song?" Paintings can be viewed without regard to their specific message or subject matter; musical compositions can be treated without the help of title or the composer's written intention. One could discuss, for example, the concept of mass in visual art by placing side by side the *Self-Portrait* (seated) of Rembrandt and *Monsieur Boileau au Cafe* of Toulouse-Lautrec. Or, analyze the treatment of melody in Brubeck, Gregorian Chant, and Bach.

So long as this approach is pursued within the same form of art, there is little trouble. However, because of the similarity of vocabulary in the arts, many people prefer to broaden their scope to include diverse art forms. Thus, people speak of how "colorful" Berlioz's music is, or Coleridge's "tone color," or the "thick texture" of Wallace Stevens, or the "space" in Copland's compositions. It should be kept in mind, however, that a musical line, a poetic line, and a painter's line are not equivalent. Picasso's handling of a single, unbroken pencil line is wholly different from a long drawn Bach melody. Nonetheless, many allied arts teachers treat such a term—*line*—as though it means the same thing in the different art forms. Can one truly compare the west façade of a Gothic cathedral with a random musical composition in ternary form? Or are the advocates of the elements approach really speaking of artistic *principles*? The persistent question is this: *Are* these examples comparable?

Many writers advise us to concentrate upon the uniqueness of each art, and not upon how we might contrive to interrelate or compare them. Those who favor the elements approach cannot escape the charge that elements do vary from one art form to another; we really should not gloss over all the differences simply by using a common vocabulary.

Artistic Principles

We seek an approach that is relatively easy to put into practice, one that considers both the uniqueness of each art and the affinity each art seems to have with the others. Every approach suggested so far has its opponents as well as advocates. Our needs seem so simple: How can the use of nonmusical arts in our lessons help to increase our students' artistic perception, sensitivity, and appreciation?

Let us consider the benefits of using *artistic principles* as our framework. Are there basic principles and means evident in all the arts, no matter when or where they were created? If we examine jointly a Greek amphora, a Gothic cathedral, a Renaissance madrigal, a Watteau canvas, a Coleridge poem, and a Brancusi bronze, is it possible that we might discover some underlying similarities? Obviously, the materials (clay, stone, tones, pigment, words, and metal) differ, so we cannot get very far comparing them; their place in history certainly is different, so we should not draw any conclusions from that. Purpose, function, and subject matter clearly are not similar. We must look past these differences to things more basic.

Each of these examples exhibits the artistic principles of *unity* and *variety*. These principles are applied through the means of *repetition* and *contrast*. Each example, of course, presents a unique embodiment of the principles. The repetition of figures on the amphora may be simply the alternation of two contrasting geometric patterns; the structural scheme of the madrigal may be more subtle. Nonetheless, each work achieves unity through the repetition and relation of parts to the whole. This is not to say that ternary song form is "the same as" the west façade of a Gothic cathedral, because both exhibit a kind of "ABA" form. Rather, the two are comparable simply in that both show the strength that derives from unity and the interest generated by variety.

The basic principles of unity and variety, developed through repetition and contrast, lead to *patterns* which contribute to the final composition. By examining and exploring these few principles in all the arts, the allied arts teacher can point out parallels while at the same time acknowledging the uniqueness of each art and each art work. Further, the sinplicity of this framework may appeal to teachers who wish to include nonmusical arts in their plans but find the strategies mentioned earlier too complicated.

The teacher's mission is to spotlight how poets, painters, sculptors, and musicians—in their unique craft, style, and art—display the characteristics of unity, variety, balance, tension, etc. You do not try to compare metaphor with pigment, or bronze with deceptive cadences. What you do point out is that unity and variety can be found and explored in just about every art work, and that each art form has a unique treatment of the artistic principles. What you compare is the principle-in-action, not two different art works. The teacher's objective—perhaps one of the most difficult facets—is to purposefully select art works from various media which clearly convey these basic principles. Even though there are myriad "masterworks," the intelligent teacher will select those that (*a*) clearly exhibit basic artistic principles, (*b*) do not offend, and (*c*) can be dealt with in a lesson with young people. Some writers and critics suggest that *anything* should be available—that to choose works with an eye toward practicality and propriety somehow denies young people their "freedom." But such a recommendation often stems from individuals who have no direct experience with teaching in the public schools.

This is not intended to imply that one should never show a slide of a Giorgione nude (for fear of offense), or that teachers should always poll the P.T.A. for what is "acceptable." Common sense should go a long way for practical considerations: Artistically, look for works that are relatively easy to analyze—that are not so abstract that students get lost along the way. Nothing will overturn an allied arts lesson faster than the use of visual arts that are overwhelmingly complex and remote. Your initial lessons using painting, architecture, sculpture or poetry must succeed in capturing the hearts and interests of your students before you can hope to make use of long-range plans of increasing difficulty.

Historical background can be both useful and worthwhile. It is only when one capsulizes periods into neat, tidy descriptions that problems arise. Nineteenth-century music is particularly given to generalizations. Students learn to expect long, gushy works for huge orchestras, or endless operatic warbling, or they expect every piece to have a fanciful title and program. Rather than attempting to narrowly define an artistic style, it might be better to discuss the purely historical, nonartistic events surrounding the works being examined. Consider the aspects of life at the time seemingly "incidental" to the arts—politics, wars, costumes, exploration, etc. Many allied arts lessons come alive because the teacher took the time to research facets of the historical period that might appeal to adolescents. Some teachers have even entered such classes dressed in period costumes—for novelty, attention, and dramatic impact.

One could doubtless discover or even invent additional avenues to the arts beyond those mentioned here. It is suggested that approaches which are primarily art work-centered are best. By using artistic principles as a framework, one can roam far and wide—from era to era, or culture to culture, or art medium to art medium—with some confidence. But how can this approach be implemented? What would an allied arts lesson based on artistic principles look like? Let us address these questions now.

THE ALLIED ARTS LESSON

Some general comments first:

1. Select carefully.
2. Make initial lessons short and captivating.

3. Do not try to "cover the material" by attempting too much—*limit your focus.*
4. Study the art works well yourself. Keep in mind that the perceptions of the class will be different from your own.
5. Nurture the aesthetic development of each person or class, rather than imposing your own views and preferences.
6. Discover and then convey aspects of the selected works that truly interest *you.* This should not serve as the "true interpretation," but rather as the honest communication of material between you and the class. Students will sense that you enjoy sharing your appreciation of nonmusical art works.
7. Be ready to encounter lack of interest from your class. Many will openly wonder why the music teacher is talking about poetry or painting. After all, they might think, shouldn't someone else deal with that?
8. When presenting visual art (slides, pictures, reproductions), take some time to let the art work speak for itself before you introduce commentary and discussion.
9. Poetry is usually the most difficult art to include because of the great variation among students in reading skill and language appreciation. Frequently, students fail to respond to "great poems" because they cannot decipher the words, inferences, and subtleties. Be especially careful in selecting poetry.
10. Allied arts lessons can be developed which are broad enough to require several days or even weeks for completion. However, it might be wise to begin by occasionally including nonmusical art works. Their inclusion should be brief, almost "incidental," yet purposeful and diverting. Publishers organize chapters or units on the various historical periods not only around music but also around painting, poetry, and so on. Too often, general music teachers avoid this readily available content and skip to the song or a recording.
11. Finally, keep in mind that good works of art follow no absolute rules or formulas. Even though some creative endeavors may clearly emphasize one artistic principle, most worthwhile art *is* worthwhile because it subtly blends various principles.
12. As with your musical choices, plan to "revisit" often the art selections you make. Middle school students show greater willingness to participate when dealing with familiar materials. Point out or discuss something different each time. Good art work calls for repeated scrutiny for full appreciation.

Allied Arts Lessons Based on Principles

These plans are conceived to span several consecutive meetings, a week or longer. Each class segment should end with a review, and each successive resumption should begin with a review.

The Allied Arts 145

LESSON PLAN 1   UNITY THROUGH REPETITION

OBJECTIVES

to observe, identify, and discuss the manner in which repetition unites each example; to note the similarities of means within each medium and the differences among media

MATERIALS

overhead projector, black paper shapes, scratch paper, score or recording:

Chopin, Prelude in E minor, Op. 28, No. 4

Dvorak, Symphony in E minor, Op. 95, 2nd movement

slide or print:
Riley, *Current* (painting)
Coliseum or Parthenon (architecture)
Cubi XVIII, David Smith (sculpture)
Hammarskjold, *Markings* (poetry)

Introduction

"We begin with something very simple: six toothpick lines on the board." On the board, mark | | | | | | . "Six equal, straight lines. They don't look like much, but it will surprise you how the way they are arranged can make you feel. For example, suppose I arrange the six like this [erase and make them ||| | ∕—]. Does that arrangement make you feel something has happened? Can you feel movement or activity? Now, can you arrange the six so that the feeling is one of rest—of no movement or activity?" Let students work at the board and on scratch paper. "Now, can you arrange them into a pattern or form that simply repeats itself?" Look for something like the original | | | | | | or ⁼ ⁼⁼, for example. Again, use board volunteers and seat work. "By putting the lines in the same direction or in pairs, we create a pattern that *repeats*. All art uses the idea of repetition because it makes the eye or ear comfortable—it unites the art work."

Musical Example

"Listen to this familiar piece and tell me *what repeats again and again,* the top or bottom part?

(Segue).

"No matter what I do on top, the bass line repeats over and over, and this repetition holds the piece together. Music uses patterns of notes repetitiously to unite a work. Now, let's examine something else. Look at this picture and tell me what idea or part or motif holds the picture together."

Art Example: Bridget Riley, *Current*

"Before you answer, let your eye move about; look at the edge, the center, the whole. Does it do anything to you? Can you figure out where the repetition is? Keep in mind the work we did earlier with the toothpicks." Get class response. "See how the one-line idea repeats in such a way that it creates a pattern, one that has a strange effect on the eyes.

"Now, let's move to another example. For this one, I won't help you. Read it silently and be able to tell me where repetition is."

Poetry example: Dag Hammarskjold, *Markings*

> The cup,
> You shall empty it.
>
> The pain,
> You shall conceal it.
>
> The truth,
> You shall be told it.
>
> The end,
> You shall endure it![5]

Don't hurry through this. Give vocabulary aid where needed. Lead students to notice the couplet form of the repetition of pattern in both lines. "Does it rhyme? Does it have to? What mood is created? How?

"Our next example may look familiar to some of you. It's the Coliseum in Rome. Just as we have places called the Coliseum today for sports events, so in those ancient days this building was the place for gladiator fights and public spectacles. Our picture shows the outside. Look at it, and then on your scratch paper draw the part or parts you see repeating over and over. Don't hurry. Look at each area closely."

Architecture example: Coliseum (Rome)

Move about the class and look for students who render, even crudely, the pattern of arches and pillars, or arches atop other arches, or the series of pilasters. After a short interval, let individuals go to the screen and point to whatever they conclude is the repetitive motif. How would it look if each arch were a different size?

"We have dealt with four examples. Each was held together by the repetition of some part of it. What did we decide repeated in

---

5. From Dag Hammarskjold, *Markings*, trans. Leif Sjoberg and W. H. Auden (New York: Alfred A. Knopf, 1966), p. 201. Used with permission.

1. the music [bass line pattern]?
2. the painting [single curvy line]?
3. the poem [pairs of lines, pattern of nouns, and 'You shall _____ it']?
4. the building [arches, pillars, floor to floor]?

"Let's see if we can say all this in a simpler way. We found repetition in music in the pattern of [notes]; we found repetition in painting in the pattern of [lines]; we found repetition in poetry in the pattern of [words]; we found repetition in architecture in the pattern of [shapes]. Each example had form and unity because some simple part of each was repeated. But, would you say all four are the same? Why not? Repetition is different in each art, but the *idea* of repetition is common to them all.

"Our first four examples were fairly clear. The part or parts that repeated stood out easily. But most music, painting, poetry and architecture is not quite so simple. Many works have more than one idea or motif repeating. Usually, repetition is not exactly the same time after time; it isn't always the bass line in music, or one line in painting. So don't expect repetition in art to always jump out at you and yell 'Here I am!' The next set of examples presents repetition, but you will need sharp ears and eyes.

"Listen to this short section from a piano prelude by Chopin. Let your attention switch from top part to lower part and back, and see if you can name *two* things or ideas or patterns that seem to repeat. I'll play it twice."

Music example: Chopin, Prelude in E minor,
Op. 28, No. 4 (first eight measures)

If response is slow or confused, separate right- and left-hand lines and replay. Look for the identification of (*a*) left-hand chords, (*b*) left-hand rhythm, (*c*) right-hand rhythm, (*d*) same chord in left played four times and then changed, and (*e*) two-note right-hand pattern for four measures and repeated lower in measures 5–8. If possible, use an opaque projector or copy the eight measures on an acetate overhead sheet, and let the class see the score. Point out how the various parts repeat, and replay.

"Remember our first music example? That four-note idea in the bass repeated over and over and was easy to pick out. But the one we just looked at and heard had all sorts of repetition. We discovered that notes can repeat in a pattern, that rhythm patterns can help hold a piece together, and that musical ideas can repeat higher or lower. All these things are important in music. Artists have to choose what things they want to repeat, and then arrange them in imaginative ways. That bass line in our first example would get tiresome after a while without changes, repeated over and over exactly the same. Good art possesses repetition in ways that listeners and viewers enjoy time and again.

148 Lesson Plan 1   Unity Through Repetition

"Let's experiment, not with notes but with simple shapes. On your scratch paper, I'd like to have you draw the seven shapes here on the board. Use the same dimensions shown, and draw them so that each shape touches another one. Develop something you like. I'll ask some of you to come up and copy your idea using these same shapes on the overhead projector." On the board, draw these shapes:

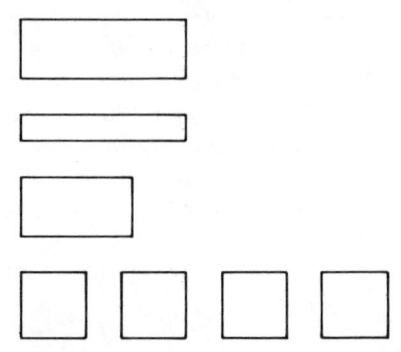

Approximate these shapes with opaque black paper, and have them ready at the overhead projector. Go around the class and spot inventive arrangement. Ask certain students to go up and arrange the black shapes on the projector the same way they drew them at their seats. Get class comments about balance, tension, interest, and so forth.

"These same shapes were used by a metal sculptor. Let's look at David Smith's *Cubi XVIII.*" Show slide or picture. "Note that repetition here is not exact. The shapes are not all the same size; they are not all arranged in the same direction. Smith's arrangement has a special quality or 'feel' about it, just as yours do. You all worked with the same shapes, yet look how different your compositions are.

"We'll conclude our work on repetition for now by returning to some music. We have seen that all the arts use repetition—that repeating ideas, words, shapes or notes helps keep things together, like cement. But we have seen that even with much repetition, we need some contrast to add interest. We arrange sentences or arches or squares or note patterns so that they don't become monotonous. Good listeners and 'art watchers' look for little differences. We'll see if you can do that right now. The music we will hear has six short parts or phrases to it. To help you listen, here's a guide with numbers and questions. I'll play the music twice; first, just follow the guide as I call the numbers. Don't mark anything. The second time, though, as I call each number, circle the answer that seems correct to you."

Music example: Dvorak, Symphony In E Minor, Op. 95,
                      second movement, opening theme in English Horn
                      (twelve measures only)

Number	Questions About the Melody	
1	phrase A (the original; no answer needed)	
2	exactly the same?	slightly different?
3	phrase A?	phrase B?
4	exactly the same?	different?
5	phrase A?	phrase B?
6	exactly the same?	different?

        There are two pairs of exact repetition:
                numbers____and____,
                numbers____and____.

Discuss the students' answers to this short quiz. To reinforce their perception, isolate the theme for one-finger piano performance. Comment phrase by phrase, and then replay the original at the end. Exchange papers, or use self-grading. Show the score—melody only if possible. Let the eye help the ear. Consider graphing the melody as it plays.

150 Lesson Plan 1 Unity Through Repetition

"We have dealt with *repetition in art*. We have seen it in the Coliseum, poetry, painting, sculpture, and music. Repetition serves what purpose? Why don't artists just repeat ideas over and over exactly the same each time? Repetition ⟶ Unity. Repetition is all around us. When we meet again, tell us at least one thing in your house that shows repetition, either exact or slightly different."

Depending on the class ability and interest, you may wish to either substitute or supplement the earlier examples with these:

Art
Tower of Blue Horses by Franz Marc
Revolt of the Aqueducts by Paul Klee
Broadway Boogie Woogie by Piet Mondrian

Literature
"African Dance" by Langston Hughes
"Keep a'Goin' " by Frank Stanton
"I Have a Dream" by Martin L. King, Jr.
"The Raven" by Edgar A. Poe

Architecture
St. Pierre (Moissac), central portal tympanum
Amiens Cathedral, west facade

Music
Haydn's Symphony No. 104, fourth movement, opening
Bach's Two-Part Inventions, 8, 10

STUDENT PLAN   UNITY THROUGH REPETITION

(worksheet to be filled in by student teacher)

OBJECTIVES

to review ideas generated in previous lesson; to reexamine some of the music/art slides/poetry and introduce new examples; to develop a short audiovisual test for class to determine students' grasp of the idea of repetition

MATERIALS

STUDENT PLAN   UNITY THROUGH REPETITION
(student teacher worksheet, continued)

STUDENT PLAN STRENGTH CONVEYED BY THE REPETITION OF VERTICAL PATTERNS

(worksheet to be filled in by student teacher)

OBJECTIVES

to suggest that the repetition of aural/visual patterns can convey strength; to explore through classroom activities how this may be achieved through aural/visual emphasis upon the vertical

MATERIALS

Moussorgsky, *Pictures at an Exhibition* (Promenade)
Hindemith, *Mathis der Maler,* III (conclusion)
Ictinus and Callicrates, *Parthenon*
Gainsborough, *Mrs. Graham*

STUDENT PLAN   **STRENGTH CONVEYED BY THE REPETITION OF VERTICAL PATTERNS**

(student teacher worksheet, continued)

LESSON PLAN 2   MOTION IN ART

MATERIALS

Nude Descending a Staircase #2 by Duchamp

OBJECTIVES

to observe, identify, and discuss the manner in which motion or movement is conveyed in art; to note the infinite variety of the quality of this motion from art to art

Introduction

"Do you remember when we used those six toothpick lines to create a feeling of repetition? How we first put the lines like this ||/// __ to show how an idea can be conveyed simply? Today, I want you to arrange another set of six stick-lines on your scratch paper to give a feeling of tension, or activity, or restlessness. See what you can do on your own." If you wish, use other drawings, such as . Share as many ideas from the class as possible. Put some on the board, or use the overhead projector again with the black paper strips. "In all the sketches or arrangements which seem active or tense, can we find any basic 'rules' or features that apply to them all? Could we say something like this: 'drawings that seem tense or restless usually have lines or shapes that. . . .' " Let the *class* develop a working definition or description. "Let's see if your definition holds true in this painting:"

Nude Descending Staircase #2 (1912) by Duchamp

"The idea was not to make it look realistic; the artist tried to capture the *idea* of movement down some stairs. Was it successful? Are shapes or lines repeated? Do shapes overlap? Does a sense of movement in visual art need repetition? Can you trace on scratch paper the basic lines of this painting? Does that help you sense the feeling of motion?" Supplement this with as many of the following as you need to help the class test its working definition:

> Laocoon group (150 B.C.)
> *The Parable of the Blind* (1568) by Brueghel
> *The Blessed Ludovica Albertoni* (1674) by Bernini
> *Lion Hunt* (1861) by Delacroix
> *Stag at Sharkey's* by Bellows
> *Autumn Rhythm* (1950) by Pollock
> *Construction 8* (1954) by Rivera

With each new work shown, be quiet first to let the art work speak directly to the class. Avoid lecturing and pointless talk. Phrase your questions carefully. Focus the class' attention on all aspects: line, shapes, arrangement, repetition, contrast, color, and so on. Is it only line that conveys movement? What about color? If you want to try a novel approach, trace an older painting in simple outline fashion on clear acetate and project it via the overhead apparatus. Then experiment with felt-tip markers, trying various color combinations. Are they as successful as the original? Or trace the outline on a ditto master and reproduce copies for the class to experiment with at their desks.

"Let's return to our toothpick sticks. How would you arrange them now to create a feeling of movement, of tension? Can we stay with our first description or definition for tension/movement/unrest in visual art? Do you think any of our first ideas should be changed?

"So far, we have talked about movement in pictures and shapes and drawings. Does music have movement? You can't 'see' music the way you see a picture, but we do sense motion in music. What is there in music that gives this feeling—the melody? Beat? Harmony? Everything? Let's see.

"Can we apply our description to fit music? With some rewording, we could say that music has motion or movement or gives us a sense or feel of unrest when. . . ." Again, have the class decide on some definition. Your aim is to elicit some discussion about how music can be arranged to give a sense of restlessness. Your ability to improvise is particularly important now. If discussion lags, spark the students' imagination with something like what is shown in Figure 8.2.

"The same tune, played twice, and at the same speed. Did one seem to have more motion or activity than the other? Why? Should we add this idea to our working definition of musical movement? Consider the *quality* of the motion. Note, too, that dynamics play an important part in determining the quality or 'feel' of the musical motion. Active but quiet compositions have an entirely different quality about them than active, noisy pieces. Clearly, good composers know this and select the dynamic level that best suits their intentions." Play both again, altering speed and dynamics.

"We have noted that the presence or absence of regularity in movement is important to the quality of that movement. Rhythms that are persistent and unvarying, as in much of popular music, set up predictable expectations; we hear the strong, regular accents and we sense motion that might be described as driving, strong, active. Conversely, rhythms that are irregular or shifting or without accent patterns can make us feel unsettled or edgy or even downright uncomfortable." Consider using any of the following as additional examples of irregular rhythms and meters:

The Allied Arts   157

FIGURE 8.2

What about this?

and this?

and this:

or consider:

(any drum)   (no accents)

or. . .   or

Consider these two:

G   D   G   D

Lesson Plan 2 Motion in Art

Dupré, Passion Symphonie ("The World Awaiting the Saviour")
Stravinsky, Le Sacre du Printemps
  L'Histoire du Soldat
Bartok, Music for Strings, Percussion, and Celesta

"All art has some sort of motion. Certainly, some very modern examples—a canvas all one solid color, for instance—seem to go against this idea. But almost every example we see or hear or read has some movement. And the quality of this movement is unique to each art work. The presence of regular patterns tends to make us contented; irregularity in any art work makes us uncomfortable. Motion or movement is affected by more than just pattern: speed, dynamics, tone color, palette color, texture, material, and so on. All affect the quality of the perceived motion. Thus, to reproduce Rivera's *Construction 8* in rough, weathered iron would produce an effect different from that of the original. Being aware of and sensitive to these many variations available to artists will make us better appreciators."

STUDENT PLAN   MOTION IN ART

(worksheet to be filled in by student teacher)

OBJECTIVES	MATERIALS (suggested)
to review ideas from previous lesson; to reexamine music/slides/poetry and introduce new examples	Coleridge, "Christabel" (opening) Tintoretto, *Last Supper* Delacroix, *Death of Sardanapalus* Orozco, *Los Zapatistas*

STUDENT PLAN   MOTION IN ART
(student teacher worksheet, continued)

LESSON PLAN 3 REPOSE IN ART

OBJECTIVES

to observe, identify, and discuss the manner in which repose (or rest or stasis) is conveyed in art; to note the factors which contribute to this feeling

MATERIALS (suggested only)

ART
Early Sunday Morning by Hopper
Theodora and Retinue—mosaic at St. Vitale
Water Meadows near Salisbury by Constable
Last Supper by da Vinci
Madame Recamier by David
Landscape with Ruins by Ruisdael
Any Buddha figures

POETRY
"Chamber Music XXXV" by James Joyce

MUSIC
Diptyque (last half) by Messiaen
Concerto No. 2 in B♭ major for Piano and Orchestra, Movement II—opening by Brahms
Messiah ("Pastorale Symphony") by Handel
Symphony No. 2 in E minor, Adagio (clarinet theme) by Rachmaninoff

STUDENT PLAN   REPOSE IN ART

(worksheet to be filled in by student teacher)

OBJECTIVES

to prepare a lesson similar to the previous ones, with introduction, content, activities, and review

MATERIALS

STUDENT PLAN   REPOSE IN ART

(student teacher worksheet, continued)

Conclusion

It should be apparent now that the whole idea of allying the arts seems easy and yet complex. Experts in the arts cannot agree even on whether or not to attempt the alliance, much less as to how it should be done. That should not hold you back you from pursuing this idea in music class. Certainly, your primary purpose is to develop *musical* awareness and skills in your students. Nevertheless, including nonmusical arts as part of your musical curriculum will support the work of your art department colleagues and also enhance your own program.

Even if your only effort along these lines is reflected in the bulletin board material you select, you still will be showing sensitivity to and concern for the arts. Get some inexpensive art prints from the local museum or bookstore, changing them from time to time for a visual "treat" in your classroom. Refer to these prints when appropriate to your music lesson. Discuss the art program with the art teacher in your building; find ways for you two to support each other's efforts.

In brief, no matter how you choose to include other arts:

1. Select carefully.
2. Use the best examples you can locate.
3. Focus always on the artistic aspect and downplay the background data.
4. Allow students time to examine works.
5. Allow students to develop their own opinions and to ask questions.
6. Avoid complex works and inappropriate vocabulary in your selections.
7. Aim for diversity and variety rather than limiting examples only to those particular things *you* like.

Questions & Activities

1. Examine any source in the library intended as an allied arts resource and determine its underlying approach or philosophy. Note in particular the comments in the preface.
2. In addition to the traditional themes selected by artists, identify yet another "theme" which has drawn the attention of at least three artists, and present the theme and examples to the class.
3. Select a typical Renaissance painting—perhaps a scene with three or four persons—and try, using pencil and paper, to rearrange the figures. Even if your drawing skills seem quite amateur, try to block in placement

and dimensions for the persons and background. Compare your variations to the original, and discuss.

4. Compile lists of accessible materials (recordings, prints, poems, etc.) that seem appropriate to young people. Share your research with the class.
5. Report on the resources available in the community. Besides the local art museum, hunt out small sidewalk galleries and shops that provide examples of art either for observation or purchase. Share your information (perhaps by a handout) with the class.
6. Present to the class a short lesson which compares two works either from the same medium or from two different areas.
7. Select *one* example of visual art, either a slide or a large reproduction. Have groups or individuals present a short lesson on this work, adopting any one of the approaches mentioned in this chapter. If possible, schedule three or four presentations during the same class meeting, to invite discussion and comparison.
8. Invite a representative from the school/university art department to visit your class and discuss problems and approaches.
9. Assign students the task of creating imaginative bulletin board layouts which center upon a topic or theme relevant for allied arts work.

Appendix A
Publishers and Firms

The following publishers and firms produce materials that are appropriate for general music classes and may interest teachers of such classes:

Addison-Wesley Publishing Company, 2725 Sand Hill Road, Menlo Park, Calif. 94025.
American Book Company, 135 West 50th Street, New York, N.Y. 10020.
ARP Instruments, Inc., 45 Hartwell Avenue, Lexington, Mass. 02173.
Bowmar/Noble Publishers, Inc., 4563 Colorado Blvd., Los Angeles, Calif. 90039.
Michael Brent Publications, Box 1186, Port Chester, N.Y. 10573.
The Corinthian Press, 3592 Lee Road, Shaker Heights, Oh. 44120.
Creative Audio Visuals, 11820 Edgewater, Cleveland, Oh. 44107.
EAV, Inc.-Educational Audio Visual, Pleasantville, N.Y. 10570.
Follett Publishing Company, 1010 West Washington Blvd., Chicago, Ill. 60607.
GAMT Music Press, P. O. Box 125, Jamestown, R.I. 02835.
Charles Hansen Music & Books, Inc., 1860 Broadway, New York, N.Y. 10023.
Holt, Rinehart & Winston, Inc., 383 Madison Avenue, New York, N.Y. 10017.
Hope Publishing Company, Carol Stream, Ill. 60187.
Houghton Mifflin Company, One Beacon Street, Boston, Mass. 02107.
Keyboard Publications, 1346 Chapel Street, New Haven, Conn. 06511.
Macmillan Publishing Co., Inc., 866 Third Avenue, New York, N.Y. 10022.
Magnamusic-Baton, 10370 Page Industrial Boulevard, St. Louis, Mo. 63132.
Malmark, Inc., Bellcraftsmen, 100 Doyle Street, Doylestown, Pa. 18901.

Music Education Group, 20 Stern Avenue, Springfield, N.J. 07081.

Music Educators National Conference, 1902 Association Drive, Reston, Va. 22091.

The World of Peripole, Inc., P. O. Box 146, Lewistown Road, Browns Mills, N.J. 08015.

Pop Hits Publications, 3149 Southern Avenue, Memphis, Tenn. 38111.

Prentice Hall Media/Jam Handy, 150 White Plains Road, Tarrytown, N.Y. 10591.

Rhythm Band, Inc., P.O. Box 126, Fort Worth, Tx. 76101.

Schulmerich Carillons, Inc., Carillon Hill, Sellersville, Pa. 18960.

Scientific Music Industries, 823 South Wabash Avenue, Chicago, Ill. 60605.

Silver Burdett Company, Morristown, N.J. 07960.

Appendix B
Allied Arts Resources

Comparison and contrast are powerful teaching techniques that are especially well suited for the allied arts. Readers may wish to consider some of the following resources.

Comparison/Contrast of Literature Set to Music

Barber
> *Knoxville: Summer of 1915*
> (poem by James Agee)

Carter
> *Heart Not So Heavy As Mine*
> (poem by Emily Dickinson)

Debussy
> *Blessed Damozel*
> (poem by Dante Rossetti)
> *Afternoon of a Faun*
> ("Eclogue" by Mallarmé)

Delius
> *Sea Drift*
> (poem "Out of the Cradle" by Walt Whitman)
> *Songs of Farewell*
> ("Leaves of Grass" by Whitman)

Hindemith
: *Six Chansons*
(poem by Rainer Maria Rilke)

Jenkins
: *Song of the Silent Land*
(poem by Longfellow)

La Montaine
: *Songs of the Rose of Sharon*
(*The Bible*, Book of Solomon, chapter 2)

Poulenc
: *Le Bal Masque*
(poems by Max Jacob)

Ravel
: *Sheherazade,* ("L'Indifference")
("The Indifferent" by Donne)

Stravinsky
: *In Memoriam Dylan Thomas* (1954)
("Do Not Go Gentle . . ." Dylan Thomas)
Three Shakespeare Songs (1953)
  "Music to Hear"
  "Full Fathom Five"
  "When Daisies Pied"

Williams, Ralph Vaughan
: *Serenade to Music*
(*Merchant of Venice*, last act, scene 1)
Toward the Unknown Region
("Whispers of Heavenly Death" by Whitman)
Three Shakespeare Songs (Chorus)
  "Full Fathom Five"
  "Cloud Capped Towers"
  "Over Hill, Over Dale"
Hodie, Part III
("*It was the winter wild . . .*" from
"Hymn on the Morning of Christ's
Nativity" by Milton)
Dona Nobis Pacem
("Beat, Beat Drums," "Word Overall,"
"Dirge for Two Veterans" by Whitman)

Comparison of Works Organized by Topic

Crucifixion
: Various medieval creations coupled with works by Brueghel, Rubens, Dali, and Orozco.

David
   Sculpture by Donatello, Verrochio, Michelangelo, and Bernini
Equestrian
   Gattamelatta (Donatello), *Tribute to Coleoni* (Verrochio)
Still Life
   Works by Zurbaran, Chardin, and Cezanne
Last Supper
   Works by Leonardo da Vinci, Tintoretto, Tiepolo, and Dali
Mood of Loneliness
   L'Absinthe (Degas), *City Square* (Giacometti), *Night Hawks* (Hopper)
Gesture
   Augustus of Prima Porta and *Man Pointing* (Giacometti, 1947)

References for the Allied Arts

Baker, Rachel. *All About Art.* New Haven: Fine Arts Publications, 1971.

Clark, Kenneth. *Civilization.* New York: Harper and Row, 1969.

Cross, Neal M.; Lamm, Robert C.; and Turk, Rudy H. *The Search for Personal Freedom.* 4th Ed. Dubuque: Wm. C. Brown Company, 1972.

Drew, Elizabeth. *Discovering Poetry.* New York: W. W. Norton & Company, 1933.

Dudley, Louise, and Faricy, Austin. *The Humanities.* 4th ed. New York: McGraw-Hill, 1967.

Eastman, Arthur M., ed. *The Norton Anthology of Poetry.* New York: W. W. Norton and Company, 1970.

Fleming, William. *Arts and Ideas.* 3d. ed. New York: Holt, Rinehart and Winston, 1968.

Gettings, Fred. *The Meaning and Wonder of Art.* New York: Golden Pleasure Books, 1963.

Gingrich, Donald. *Relating the Arts.* New York: The Center for Applied Research in Education, 1974.

Gombrich, E. H. *The Story of Art.* 12th ed. London: Phaidon Press Ltd., 1972.

Hunter, J. Paul, ed. *The Norton Introduction to Literature: Poetry.* New York: W.W. Norton and Company, 1973.

Janson, H. W. *History of Art.* Englewood Cliffs: Prentice-Hall, Inc., and New York: Harry N. Abrams, Inc., 1962.

Karel, Leon C. *Avenues to the Arts.* 2d ed. Kirksville, Mo.: Simpson Publishing Co., 1969.

Landis, Beth. *Exploring Music: The Senior Book.* New York: Holt, Rinehart and Winston, 1969.

Levey, Michael. *A History of Western Art.* New York: Frederick A. Praeger, Publishers, 1968.

———. *A Concise History of Painting.* New York: Frederick A. Praeger, Publishers, 1962.

Morman, Jean. *Art: of Wonder and a World.* Blauvelt, New York: Art Education, Inc., 1967.

Myers, Bernard S. *Art and Civilization.* 2d ed. New York: McGraw-Hill Book Company, 1967.

Newton, Eric. *The Arts of Man.* Greenwich, Conn.: New York Graphic Society, 1960.

Sachs, Curt. *The Commonwealth of Art.* New York: W. W. Norton & Company, 1946.

Scholl, Sharon, and White, Sylvia. *Music and the Culture of Man.* New York: Holt, Rinehart and Winston, 1970.

Van de Bogart, Doris. *Introduction to the Humanities.* New York: Barnes and Noble, 1968.

Wallace, Robert, and Taaffe, James G. *Poems on Poetry.* New York: E. P. Dutton and Co., 1965.

Wold, Milo, and Cykler, Edmund. *An Introduction to Music and Art in the Western World.* 4th ed. Dubuque: Wm. C. Brown Company, 1972.

Additional Sources

"Art and Man": a multi-media school program. Also available: forty slide lectures, six films, fifteen traveling exhibits. Contact The Extension Service, National Gallery of Art, Washington, D. C. 20565.

Art appreciation program: Forty-eight large prints (28" x 22") available through Art Education, Inc., Blauvelt, N.Y. 10913.

Classics of the world's great art: Individual paperbacks on specific artists are available through Harry N. Abrams, Inc., 110 E. 59th St., New York, N.Y. 10022.

Barnes & Noble Art Series: Barnes & Noble, Inc., 105 Fifth Ave., New York, N.Y. 10003.

The Colour Library of Art: Contact the Hamlyn Publishing Group Ltd., Hamlyn House, Feltham, Middlesex, England.

Design Magazine (for Arts in Education): The Saturday Evening Post Company, 1100 Waterway Boulevard, P.O. Box 567B, Indianapolis, Ind. 46206.

Skira Paperbacks: Individual paperbacks on specific artists with biographical information. Contact The World Publishing Co., 2231 W. 110th St., Cleveland, Oh. 44102.

The New Grosset Art Library: Grosset & Dunlap, Inc., 51 Madison Avenue, New York, N.Y. 10010.

Appendix C
Additional Questions and Activities

1. For general music, which is more important—breadth or depth?
2. Can you think of any musical selections that would *not* be appropriate for the general music class? Explain.
3. What is your definition of "general" music? Can you think of another title that would be better?
4. Let us suppose your school adopts a modular schedule scheme. Discuss how you might re-plan your work so that your goals could be reached within the somewhat erratic 15–20 minute modules. What requests would you make of your principal so that your musical desires would be fulfilled?
   Investigate the advantages and drawbacks to modular scheduling. How do music classes profit or lose?
5. Obtain a school curriculum outline from a local school system. Observe the wording of goals of the music program and the manner in which the goals are to be implemented. Compare these with your own. Could you work within such a system? How might you approach the superintendent to alter or re-word the printed goals?
6. What might you do if:
   a. a student falls asleep frequently in your class?
   b. a consistently tardy pupil says his last-period teacher always detains him?
   c. a pupil, on being reprimanded, weeps profusely in front of the rest of the class?
   d. Johnny always asks to go to the restroom halfway through your class?
   e. all the boys sit in the back rows and talk continually?

7. Examine the seventh and eighth grade volumes from as many series as possible. List the strengths and weaknesses of each publication. If appropriate, divide the class into small groups, each group given the assignment of preparing a short "sales" presentation for the others.
8. Assign certain students to call local middle schools and find out what kinds of equipment are available for use. If possible, have callers find out how often the music teacher signs out such equipment as overhead projectors, slides, etc.
9. Prepare a list of available films, filmstrips, slides, etc., that seem appropriate for the general music class. Consult, in particular, the MENC Film Guide for Music Educators.
10. The back row is made up boys bigger than you. The song you chose for the class to sing meets with zero participation from that row. They say they can't hit those high notes. What will you do?
11. Sally says her aunt gave her an Orff xylophone for her birthday, and she'd like to bring it to class. Bill thinks that's dumb because "that's kid's stuff," and he has had it up to here with third-grade music routines. Respond.
12. In addition to the ways suggested, how might you incorporate the use of keyboard, tone bars, Orff instruments, autoharp, guitar, and so on, into your lessons? Compile lists of possible uses for each.
13. Mr. Quaver, the music teacher, awards the best disciplined student in class with a copy of Copland's *What to Listen for in Music*. Comment on this, and consider the whole idea of giving tangible rewards for achievements.
14. Using as few and as simple words/terms as possible, prepare a short explanation, to be given in class, of the following:
    a. the musical phrase
    b. syncopation
    c. pentatonic scale
    d. how a trumpet works
    e. overtone series
    f. how a pipe organ works
    g. 12-tone technique
    h. ternary form

Appendix D
Bibliography

Andrews, Frances. *Junior High School General Music*. Englewood Cliffs: Prentice-Hall, 1971.

Bemberger, Jeanne, and Brofsky, Howard. *The Art of Listening*. New York: Harper & Row, 1972.

Bernstein, Leonard. *The Joy of Music*. New York: Simon & Schuster, 1959.

Bessom, Malcolm E.; Tatarunis, Alphonse M.; and Forcucci, Samuel L. *Teaching Music in Today's Secondary Schools*. New York: Holt, Rinehart and Winston, Inc., 1974.

Brace, Geoffrey, and Burton, Ian. *Listen! Music and Nature*. Cambridge: Cambridge University Press, 1976.

Bruner, Jerome S. *The Process of Education*. New York: Vintage Books (a division of Random House), 1960.

Cooper, Irvin, and Kuersteiner, Karl O. *Teaching Junior High School Music*. 2nd ed. Boston: Allyn & Bacon, 1970.

Dallin, Leon. *Listener's Guide to Musical Understanding*. Dubuque: Wm. C. Brown Company, 1965.

Dwyer, Terence. *Teaching Musical Appreciation*. London: Oxford University Press, 1967.

Ernst, Karl D., and Gary, Charles L. *Music in General Education*. Washington, D. C.: MENC, 1965.

Hoffer, Charles. *Teaching Music in the Secondary Schools*. Belmont, Calif.: Wadsworth Publishing Company, 1964.

Hughes, William O. *Planning for Junior High School General Music*. Belmont, Calif.: Wadsworth Publishing Company, 1964.

Langer, Suzanne K. *Problems of Art*. New York: Charles Scribner's Sons, 1957.

Lasker, Henry. *Teaching Creative Music in Secondary Schools*. Boston: Allyn and Bacon, 1971.

Leach, Robert, and Palmer, Roy, eds. *Folk Music in School*. Cambridge: Cambridge University Press, 1978.

Marple, Hugo D. *Backgrounds and Approaches to Junior High Music*. Dubuque: Wm. C. Brown Company, 1975.

Meyer, Leonard B. *Music, the Arts, and Ideas*. Chicago: The University of Chicago Press, 1967.

Monsour, Sally, and Perry, Margaret. *A Junior High School Music Handbook*. 2nd ed. Englewood Cliffs: Prentice-Hall, 1970.

Mursell, James L. Educational Psychology. New York: W. W. Norton & Company, 1939.

Paynter, John, and Aston, Peter. *Sound and Silence*. Cambridge: Cambridge University Press, 1970.

Reimer, Bennett. *A Philosophy of Music Education*. Englewood Cliffs: Prentice-Hall, 1970.

Schwadron, Abraham A. *Aesthetics: Dimension for Music Education*. Washington, D. C.: MENC, 1967.

Singleton, Ira, and Anderson, Simon V. *Music in Secondary Schools*. Boston: Allyn and Bacon, 1969.

Sur, William, and Schuller, Charles F. *Music Education for Teen-Agers*. 2nd ed. New York: Harper and Row, 1966.

Swanson, Fredrick J. *Music Teaching in the Junior High and Middle School*. New York: Appleton-Century-Crofts, 1973.

Vulliamy, Graham, and Lee, Ed. *Pop Music in School*. Cambridge: Cambridge University Press, 1976.

Wilson, A. Verne. *Design for Understanding Music*. Evanston, Ill.: Summy-Birchard Company, 1966.

Wink, Richard L., and Williams, Lois G. *Invitation to Listening*. Boston: Houghton Mifflin Co., 1972.

Winn, Cyril. *Teaching Music*. London: Oxford University Press, 1963.

Index

Aesthetic education, 4, 134–35, 139
Allied arts, 133–65
    approaches, 136–41
Areas of musical learning, 10–12
Assessment of students, 12–13
    initial test, 14–16
Audio aids. *See* Classroom materials
Bells. *See* Instruments
Bernstein, Leonard, 80
Changing voice. *See* Singing
Choral music, 53–58
Classroom materials, 46–50
    opaque projector, 49–50
    overhead projector, 49–50
    record player, 46
    tape recorder, 47
Classroom organization, 27–35
    individualization, 29–32
    small group, 28–29
    whole group, 27–28
Coliseum, 145–46, 150
Composition, 64–66
Contracts, 29–32
Curriculum, 9–25
    long-range goals, 10–12
    short-term objectives, 16–18, 77

Curriculum (cont)
    spiral, 23–25
    unit plan, 18–22
Dancing. *See* Movement
Discipline, 32–34
Discovery learning, 80
"Dona Nobis Pacem," 88
Duchamp, Marcel, 156
Expressionism, 6–7, 13
Formalism, 4–7, 12
Hammarskjold, Dag, 146–47
Handbells. *See* Instruments
Individualization. *See* Classroom
    organization
Instruments for class use, 37–46
    autoharp, 38–39
    guitar, 41–42
    handbells, 42–44
    miscellaneous, 45–46
    percussion, 39–40
    piano, 38
    recorder, 44–45
    tuned bar, 40–41
Lesson planning, 77–85
    sonata-allegro approach for, 77–81
Lesson plans, 87–130

Lesson plans (cont)
   allied arts, 145–63
      motion in art, 155–60
      unity through repetition, 145–52
   melody, 88–100
   orchestration, 108–14
   rhythm, 101–07, 118–21
   rhythm, dynamics, tone color, 122–30
Listening, 6, 70–74
Melody, 16–18, 65–66, 88–100
Movement, 66–70
Music reading, 59–64

Ostinato, 116–19
Rhythm, 101–07, 115–30, 155–60
Riley, Bridget, 145–46
Sacred Harp, 60
Sequence, 95–100
Shape notes, 59–61
Singing, 53–58
   ranges, 54–55, 58
   seating arrangement for, 57
   voice testing, 55–58
Smith, David, 145–49
Spoken fugue, 124–26